Endorsements

This is a no-B.S. guide to decoding "The Boss" and navigating various management styles to advance your career (without losing your soul). Really a "must read" for people looking to maximize their career opportunities and young professionals aspiring to accelerate their success.

—Cary Hatch, CEO, Brand Advocate
MDB Communications

As a business owner managing hundreds of personalities, Abbajay's advice and perspective is refreshing and very needed to cut through the noise of the management book genre. I cannot wait to share copies with my team and discuss how we can ALL play a role in managing a great company.

—Gina Schaefer, Founder and CEO
A Few Cool Hardware Stores/Former ACE Hardware Board Member

Abbajay's keen understanding of personality and leadership styles is unmatched! This is the book you need to read to achieve your best career possible.

—Douglas M. Duncan, President and CEO
Leadership Greater Washington

In a world where we all must be more entrepreneurial to keep pace with the rapid changes in technology and the jobs we do, *Managing Up* is an important tool kit for people looking to keep up. Leadership comes from above and below–if you know how to do it. Read this book.

—Jonathan Aberman, Managing Director
Amplifier Ventures

"A refreshing take on managing your career! No more excuses for why you're unhappy at work and can't achieve your goals. Abbajay proves you can succeed with any type of boss – you just have to ditch the drama, accept the boss you have, and understand that the only person you can change is yourself. An empowering read for employees at every stage of their career!"

—Cy Wakeman
New York Times Bestselling Author and Drama Researcher - Newest book is No Ego, How leaders can cut the cost of workplace drama, end entitlement and drive big results

"Mary Abbajay's knowledge and experience in understanding leadership styles is as extensive as it is terrific! Her advice is relevant, accurate and immediately deployable in the modern workplace."

—Jeffery M Rubery,
Washington, DC Market President, BB&T Bank

MAN^AGING
UP

MANAGING
UP

HOW TO **MOVE** UP, **WIN** AT WORK, AND
SUCCEED WITH ANY TYPE OF BOSS

MARY ABBAJAY

WILEY

Published by John Wiley & Sons, Inc., Hoboken, New Jersey.
Published simultaneously in Canada.

For general information on our other products and services or for technical support, please contact our Customer Care Department within the United States at (800) 762-2974, outside the United States at (317) 572-3993 or fax (317) 572-4002.

Wiley publishes in a variety of print and electronic formats and by print-on-demand. Some material included with standard print versions of this book may not be included in e-books or in print-on-demand. If this book refers to media such as a CD or DVD that is not included in the version you purchased, you may download this material at http://booksupport.wiley.com. For more information about Wiley products, visit www.wiley.com.

Library of Congress Cataloging-in-Publication Data is Available:

ISBN 9781119436683 (Hardcover)
ISBN 9781119436652 (ePDF)
ISBN 9781119437161 (ePub)

Cover Design: Wiley
Cover Image: © Matt_Gibson/iStockphoto

Printed in the United States of America

10 9 8 7 6 5 4 3 2 1

For my father, Duane Abbajay, a man who truly knew how to work with people – and was loved by every damn one of them

Contents

Acknowledgments

So Many People to thank. Let me start with my amazing Careerstone Group team: Carly Eckard, Chris Butts, Laura Buckley, and Nanami Hirata. Thank you for keeping the boat afloat while I ghosted on you all to write this book. You all are masters at managing me up every day. And I totally appreciate it. Keep it up.

Huge thanks to my sister, Stephanie Abbajay, who is always my first reader and biggest cheerleader. Thanks to my husband, Chris Marlow, who always supports my crazy schedule and who kept me and the dogs fed and watered throughout this process.

Thank you to Perry Hooks whose friendship, generosity, and advice were a godsend.

I owe an enormous debt of gratitude to my clients, friends, colleagues, and hundreds of workshop participants who trusted me with their stories and tales of managing up. I am deeply grateful for your openness and willingness to share your experiences. You all inspired me deeply. I hope this book does you justice.

None of this would have been possible without Jeanenne Ray and the Wiley team, who took a chance on a first-time author. Thank you.

And finally, a huge thanks to all the organizations and businesses who keep hiring and retaining people who are terrible at managing other people. Without you, there would be no need for this book. Thank you for the fodder.

About the Author

Mary Abbajay is an acclaimed public speaker, organizational consultant, and corporate train er. She is the president and founder of Careerstone Group, a professional development company that delivers leading-edge talent and organizational development solutions to Fortune 500 companies, government agencies, and non-profits. She is passionate about helping organizations create productive and positive workplaces where both the organization and individual can flourish. She lives with her husband and two dogs in Washington, DC.

Introduction

THERE ARE LITERALLY tens of thousands of books written on how to be an effective leader and manager. You heard me, *tens of thousands*. But clearly all these books haven't made too much of an impression on many managers since the number one reason people quit their jobs is still because of their boss. Year after year, studies show that the most common reason people leave their employer is due to having a bad boss or having a bad relationship with their boss.

Could there really be so many bad bosses out there? Are all these books written in some secret code that's impossible to crack? Or is it that we just don't know how to deal with difficult bosses? Could it be that we have failed to highlight and teach a far more important strategy – **how to manage those who manage us**?

Yes, it could. While there are thousands of books (and TED talks, conferences, YouTube videos, etc.) on how to lead and manage *downward*, there is very little out there on a far, far more important skill – *how to manage up*. In other words, how to be a successful follower.

There I said it. The "F" word. *Follower*. Nobody likes to think of himself as a follower. I get it. Even writing it makes me throw up a little in my mouth. In America, we love-love-love leaders. We talk incessantly about leadership. We preach it, we teach it, we hit everyone over the head with it. We are obsessed with it. But in the real world, where most of us actually live and work, we need to know how to follow, too. We need to know how to manage those who manage us (which is itself a form of leadership).

So, while we might resist the notion of being a follower, the truth is that the majority of us spend more of our working time following than leading. Even a CEO must be a follower, too. Everybody has a boss. The workplace isn't a democracy, and (unless you work for Zappos) it isn't a holacracy either (look it up). No, the real world of work requires close integration of leaders and followers. It requires cooperation and collaboration across hierarchies. It's time for us to learn how to be empowered followers, to take an active role in managing our careers, ourselves, our bosses, and our experience.

It's time to learn to manage up.

Managing Up offers proven, effective strategies to manage your manager based on personality and behavioral preferences. It's not about political persuasion or Machiavellian machinations, it's about understanding who your boss is and how they interact with the world. It's about offering you strategies and ideas to navigate specific personality and behavioral tendencies. It's not about changing your boss, it's about finding ways to understand and adapt to your boss's style. It is not about being a brownnose or sucking up, it's about subtle changes in your behavior, your choices, and your attitude that will help increase your ability to thrive and/or survive with the boss that you actually have, not the boss you wish you had.

This book is the result of 20 years of helping organizations and individuals create positive and productive workplaces. My team and I have coached, counseled, and trained thousands of people on how to better understand their workplace, better engage with their fellow employees, and develop better relationships with their bosses. This is my specialty. The strategies offered in this book are the result of real-world application from real-world people. All names have been changed to protect the innocent and the guilty.

By learning how to effectively manage those who manage you, you put yourself in the driver's seat and take control of your career. *Managing Up* offers practical, proven, real-world solutions and strategies to help you take charge and succeed. Be the leader of your own career. Learn to manage up.

1

Stop Complaining and Start Winning – Managing Up Is the Key to Your Success

"Once I gave up the hunt for villains, I had little recourse but to take responsibility for my choices . . . Needless to say, this is far less satisfying than nailing villains. It also turned out to be more healing in the end."

—Barbara Brown Taylor

Let's be clear: Managing up is not about brownnosing, sucking up, or becoming a sycophant. Managing up is about consciously and deliberatively developing and maintaining effective relationships with supervisors, bosses, and other people above you in the chain of command. It is a deliberate effort to increase cooperation and collaboration in a relationship between individuals who often have different perspectives and uneven power levels. It is about consciously working with your boss to obtain the best possible results for you, your boss, and the organization.

Managing up is about *you* taking charge of *your* workplace experience. Here's why it's the key to your success.

Your Boss Matters

As much as we would love to believe that the work world is a meritocracy, where just being great at your job is all you need to succeed, reality tells a different story. The real (and inconvenient) truth is that your boss has a great deal of influence over your career success and trajectory. Your relationship with her, and her experience with you, will determine the kinds of opportunities that come your way in your organization. **Establishing strong, productive working relationships is the single most effective way to accelerate success in any organization.** Earn your boss's trust and good things come your way; incur your boss's ire and you may find yourself out of the running for promotions and opportunities. Long story short, your relationship with your boss can hurt or help you. It's up to you.

Your Boss Isn't Going to Change

People are who they are. Your boss isn't going to change who she is or how she operates just because you would prefer her to be different. Her personality got her where she is today; his approach has been approved by the powers above him. She believes her way works. He gets rewarded for his style of managing. Or the organization doesn't see the problem or doesn't have the stomach to address it. While you can't change who they are, you can change how you interact with them, and that's where *Managing Up* comes in. By understanding what makes them tick, you can adapt strategies to create a more robust relationship. You can't change how they deal with you, but you can change how you deal with them. In an ideal world, managers and leaders would adapt to their employees. They would use adaptive relationship–based methods to produce the best results. But the truth is that only 30 percent of managers use more than one style of managing; the rest don't bother. If you work for one of the 70 percent you may be waiting a long time for things to go your way at work with your manager. Why wait? The more effective strategy is, you guessed it, to practice adaptive strategies yourself. Or in other words, managing up.

Your Career Matters

Developing an effective relationship is as much *your* responsibility as theirs. Do not fall into the trap of "my boss should be . . ." or "my boss ought to . . . " A bad or difficult boss is not an excuse for lack of effort on your part. It is *your* career that will suffer if you and your boss have a bad relationship. Your role in the relationship is to provide your boss with results and performance. You must learn the essence of good "followership." *Managing Up* will teach you how to build effective relationships with your boss, which will put you in charge of your career. You can sit back and wait for your manager to change, or you can take action, manage up, and watch your career blossom.

Everybody Has to Manage Up, So Learn to Be Good at It

Most people, whatever their title or position, spend more time and energy reporting to people *above* them than having people report *to* them, so the ability to manage up is a critical component in your career success. Whether you are reporting to a supervisor, middle manager, VP, top executive, or a board of directors, managing up is a skill that will help you develop strong relationships, which will increase cooperation, collaboration, and understanding between those who have different power levels and perspectives. It's not about brownnosing, schmoozing, or sucking up. It's about developing robust relationships with the people who have enormous influence over your career. Being able to effectively manage up is good for you, good for your boss, and good for your organization.

Choice Is Empowerment

Managing up is not about blind followership. It's about making strategic choices to obtain the best results for you, your boss, and the organization. It's the win-win-win strategy. But in order to do this, you have to come from a place of choice, not from a place of victimhood. When confronted with any difficult situation you always have three choices:

- Change the situation. (We know this is almost impossible, since we can't actually change other people and getting your boss fired is a long-term play.)
- Leave the situation. (Only you can decide when this is the best strategy, and sometimes it is.)
- Accept and adapt to the situation. (Learn to manage up!)

What isn't a choice is victimhood. Being a victim is completely disempowering. And it is a career killer and a soul killer. Don't kill your soul. It's hard to get it back.

Stop Waiting for the Unicorn and Start Working Well with the Boss You Have

Believe me, I wish bosses would be better. I wish that they would read and take to heart some of the lessons in those tens of thousands of books written on the subject. I wish that organizations would stop promoting people based on technical skills without considering their actual aptitude for managing people. I wish that bad managers would be fired. I wish that you could go to work every day and be energized, valued, inspired, and fulfilled. I also wish I could teleport myself anywhere I wanted to go. But that's not going to happen. So, unless you have a magic potion, stop waiting for the unicorn and start dealing with the boss you have. Start managing up.

Managing Up Will Make You a Better Leader

There. We've come full circle. The adaptive skills that you use to manage up will be many of the same skills you will use to manage down. If you can learn how to adapt to the needs and wants of others, to develop strong working relationships and develop win-win-win results by managing up, you will be much more equipped to do the same when you are a manager. If nothing else, you will learn what kind of manager you want to be and what kind of manager you don't want to be. Never waste the opportunity to learn from a difficult boss.

Objections to This Book

> *"Your Honor, I object!"*
>
> —Every lawyer in America

I know, I know. You have objections. People who resist managing up are full of objections. I've heard them all:

Objection 1: It's not fair.

My boss is the problem; why should I have to adapt to him? He should adapt to *me*. Yes. You are right. It's not fair. Completely and utterly not fair. But you know what else isn't fair? Life isn't fair. When given lemons, you can either sit back and suck on the sourness, bemoaning your fate, or you can take those lemons and make something out of them. Getting caught in the it's-not-fair trap is a mistake. The world is not a meritocracy and neither is the workplace. Learn to deal with it.

Objection 2: My boss needs to change, not me.

You will get no argument from me on that. I totally believe that your boss could and should learn to be a better boss. Your boss should take her job as boss seriously and do everything she can to be a boss who cares and develops her people. Your boss should understand and respect the enormity of her role. Your boss should read a book or two on being a great boss and then actually *be* a great boss. But guess what? You can't change your boss. All you can do is change your *reaction* to your boss. If your boss doesn't know how to manage people, then you have to learn to manage her.

Objection 3: Giving in only reinforces your boss's bad managerial ways.

Yes. You may be right. Adapting to your boss probably won't teach him anything about being a good boss. But neither will your animosity and resistance. As long as organizations and businesses continue to promote people based on technical skills and not people-management skills, then the odds of encountering ineffective management styles remain high. As long as organizations continue to promote people into management without providing adequate training and attention, we will have bad bosses. As long as organizations turn a blind eye to managers who crush souls, disengage employees, and ignore the importance of growing talent, we will have bad bosses. Until organizations start to place a premium on effective management styles and hold managers accountable for employee engagement, happiness, and retention, their ineffective ways will remain. So, if you work for an organization that doesn't hold managers accountable or for an organization that "doesn't get it," then please know: you can't change the culture of your organization; you can only change how you navigate it and respond to it.

Objection 4: Sucking up is for suckers

I reject the notion that managing up is the same as sucking up. I also reject the notion that sucking up is for suckers. That is misplaced pride talking. That is inflexibility talking. That is failure talking. Managing up is about adapting and building relationships. It is about learning what is important to your boss and making sure you give it to him or her – even when you think what they want is ridiculous (which it may very well be). Instead of viewing managing up as giving in or sucking up, view it as adaptive strategies for success. There is a big difference between being a spineless sycophant and being a strategic survivor and thriver. This book is about making strategic choices to help you excel, adapt, and succeed. It is not about being your boss's doormat. Excelling at managing up means keeping your ego in check and operating from a place of strategic choice, curiosity, experimentation, and openness.

Objection 5: It's the principle

Whenever I hear people defend their resistance on principle, I have to wonder. "It's the principle" usually means you are stuck on your own ego. If your boss is a discriminatory cheat or an abusive person, then you have to leave. Keeping yourself under his thumb based on "principle" is ridiculous. Unless the principle is about saving the lives of others, please know you aren't doing yourself any favors. I hope you use this book as a way to survive intact while you seek another job.

Objection 6: It's so phony!

Why should I change who I am? That feels inauthentic and fake! This objection always makes me sigh. Sigh. The thing about authenticity is that while most people think that it is a solitary action – e.g., being true to oneself or walking the talk – authenticity is actually a relational behavior. This means that to be truly authentic you must not only be comfortable with who *you* are, but you must be able to comfortably *connect* with *others* from that space.

My authentic self swears like a truck driver who hopes to be a sailor one day. Is it inauthentic when I resist dropping f-bombs during keynote speeches? No, it is not. My authentic self is extremely impatient. Am I being inauthentic when I politely allow someone to waste my time at Starbucks while they try to decide what to order?

No, it is not. My authentic self speaks rapidly and loudly. Am I being inauthentic when I slow my speech and modulate my volume? No, of course not. Authenticity is about spirit, energy, and personality. It's about bringing who you are everywhere you go. The key here is to bring the *best* of who you are everywhere you go. It's about choosing the behaviors that will allow your authentic self to successfully connect with other people. So, I save my f-bombs for friends who will appreciate them. I do my best to suppress my annoyance and impatience in public. And I try really hard to speak slowly enough for audiences who for some reason can't seem to understand my rapid speech. Being authentic does not mean you have to follow your every impulse or express every thought. It's about being in full choice about your actions. Take a cue from legendary Senate leader Mitch McConnell, who famously said, "I am the master of the unexpressed thought."

Objection 7: I can't believe you are telling me to be a patsy!
Let's be clear: This book is not about being a patsy. This book is about making choices that will enable you to thrive in the workplace. Never do anything illegal, immoral, or unethical. Whatever you decide to do, you must choose it.

I know. Some of you are thinking, "This woman is full of s**t. She's telling me to continue working for a toxic boss and just suck it up. She's an idiot." Okay, that is exactly the opposite of what this book is about. This book is about making an active choice for your career and work life. It's about not being a victim. It's about deciding what you are willing or not willing to do to be successful with your boss. It's about acting from a place of choice, *strategic* choice. And owning your choice.

If you decide you can't work for that toxic boss, then quit. And as quickly as you can manage. I'm behind you 100 percent. However, if you don't have the luxury to quit, then let's find a way to help you survive and maybe even thrive.

What I don't want you to do is to settle into victimhood. That place where you feel emotionally ravaged every day. That place where you are completely and totally emotionally and psychologically drained. That place where you have no options, no hope, and no joy. That place where you give away all your power. Because that is a bad place. That is the place where sickness and bad things happen to you mentally and physically. That is the place of ultimate emotional, physiological, and mental toxicity. *Managing Up* will help you gain control and succeed. The choice is yours.

Time to Man Up

> *"Start where you are. Use what you have. Do what you can."*
>
> —Arthur Ashe

"Man up" is my team's internal shorthand for managing up. To man up is to take responsibility for your choices, actions, and attitudes. It's about doing what needs to be done while keeping your integrity and values intact. It's about taking charge of your own experience. It's about not pointing the finger at others, but looking to see what you can do to help yourself.

In order to successfully man up, one must make a rigorous and honest analysis of the landscape of self and others. It's a simple three-step process:

1. **Assess Your Boss**

   Before you begin to manage up, you need to have a good sense of what you are managing up to. Take some time to piece together the puzzle that is your boss. Become a boss detective. Pay attention to clues she leaves. Notice who works well with your boss and how they interact with him. Look for patterns. Ask yourself the following questions:

   o What is your boss's workstyle personality? How does she interact with others?

   o How does your boss like his information? How does she prefer to communicate?

   o What are his priorities?

   o What are her goals?

   o What are his concerns, challenges, and pressures?

   o What is her experience? How did she get to where she is?

   o What is *his* boss like? What does the organization expect from her?

   o How does he like to work?

- What does she expect from you? What are her expectations for the team?
- How much does she delegate? When, to whom, how does she delegate?
- What are his pet peeves?
- What truly matters to her?

  See how many of these questions you can answer. Try to be objective and nonjudgmental. This is about gathering clues and assessing reality, not about judging. If you don't know the answers, then ask! Set up a meeting with your boss and find out. If your boss is unapproachable, ask others. It's not that hard to learn. It just takes a little effort.

2. **Assess Yourself**

   The second step is a bit harder as it requires taking a good long, honest look in the mirror. Managing up requires being brutally honest with yourself in terms of who you are, what you want, and what you need. It's also about understanding your contribution to the equation. Ask yourself the following questions:

   - What is my workstyle personality? How do I like to interact with others?
   - How do I prefer to communicate?
   - What are my priorities and goals?
   - What do I really need to operate at my best? What are my non-negotiables?
   - In what ways am I compatible with my boss? In what ways am I not?
   - Is my boss really difficult or just difficult for me? Am I the only one struggling?
   - What are my workplace strengths?
   - What are my workplace weaknesses?
   - Am I doing the job I was hired to do?
   - Is my job a good fit for me?
   - Do I bring the right attitude, energy, and motivation to be successful?
   - Would I want myself as an employee?
   - Do my coworkers think I am as great as I do?
   - How am I contributing to the situation (for better or worse)?
   - What am I resisting?

There are no right or wrong answers to the above questions. Only honest answers.

3. **Assess Your Willingness to Man Up**

Managing up is about deploying adaptive strategies, so in order to work, you must be willing to adapt. Remember, we can't change others, we can only change how we approach and interact with others. If you want your boss to adapt to you, you must be willing to adapt to her as well. Are you ready, willing, and able? Ask yourself the following questions:

o Do I like/love my job itself? Do I like/love my organization?
o Do I need this job (financially)?
o Do I need this job (for experience/career development)?
o Where am I on the scale of happiness/stress?
o Where is my boss on the scale of difficulty?
o What are the politics/organizational culture of my company? Is my boss a unicorn or is his/her style pretty indicative of the overall management style?
o Am I willing to make changes to my behavior and/or attitude?
o Am I willing to try to understand my boss?
o Do I want to thrive, solidify, or survive?
o Am I a victim?
o Can I man up? Is it worth the effort? Do I even want to try?

Remember, managing up is like putting together a puzzle. Part of the puzzle is your boss, part of it is you, and the rest of the pieces are the strategies you are willing or not willing to try. Some pieces will fit and some won't. Only you can figure out how to piece together the puzzle of your workplace experience.

Working with bosses often falls on what I call the continuum of difficulty. On the one end of the spectrum you have the Dream Boss. This is the person who totally gets you, respects you, and trusts you. You feel motivated, appreciated, and empowered. Working with this boss is a delight. You are super happy to come to work and you would do anything for this boss. In fact, you rarely think about managing up because the relationship feels natural and easy.

Scoot over to the other end of this continuum and you will find the Nightmare Boss – the boss from hell. This is the boss whose behavior is beyond the pale. Working for this person is totally soul sucking.

You dread coming to work. You walk on eggshells in her presence. The very thought of him makes you furious. Your stomach is in knots. You are eating Tums like candy. You have lost all confidence, motivation, and self-respect. You come home from work every day exhausted and demoralized. Sunday evenings feel like the night before you are to report to prison. Some days you wonder if you aren't suffering from PTSD. You don't see any light at the end of the tunnel.

Between the Dream Boss and the Nightmare Boss lie a host of other manager experiences. Some bosses may be slightly difficult for you (like the merely annoying) and some may be more difficult for you (the utterly unbearable). Understanding where you are on the continuum can help you determine your course of action.

While we will discuss strategies for the Nightmare Boss in the *Truly Terrible* chapter, the majority of this book is intended to help those who are somewhere in the middle, those who can still see some light at the end of the tunnel. Those people who are willing to take action to shift their experience, improve their relationships, and move toward a happier experience at work.

For some people, this book will help you *thrive* with your boss. You will take a good or middling relationship and transform it into a great working relationship. For others, it may only help you *survive* until you find a new job or new boss. You will (hopefully) get enough strategies to keep your sanity and soul intact until you can get out. There is no magic bullet.

Once you have a good, honest assessment of the landscape at work, your boss's attitudes and behavior, where you are on the continuum of difficulty, and your own willingness, you can start to manage up and take charge.

Ready? Let's start at square one: Is your boss an innie or outie?

2

Is Your Boss an Innie or Outie?

"The principle to remember is that all dualities and opposites are not disjoined but polar. They do not confront each other from afar; they originate in a common center."

—Michael Michalko

One of the first and best things you can do to manage up is to understand whether your boss is an introvert (an Innie) or an extrovert (an Outie) and then adapt your communication and interaction style accordingly. Why is this important? Because extroversion and introversion are core personality preferences that have an impact on two very important workplace elements: source of energy and source of communication style. Building and maintaining a successful working relationship with your boss requires communicating effectively and making sure you are working *with* their source of energy and not *against* it. In other words, are you going to be a boon to their energy level or a drain?

Understanding the Innie and Outie Preference

Introversion and extroversion are personality traits and preferences that are characterized by the following:

Source of energy

Are you energized from within (your own thoughts) or from external sources (such as other people)? Introverts energize from internal stimuli. Extroverts energize from outside stimuli.

Direction of energy

Are you focused more on the inner world of ideas and images or on the outer world of people and things? Introverts focus inward. Extroverts focus outward.

Response to external stimulation

What is the level of external stimuli that works best for you? Extroverts respond well to higher levels of external stimulation while introverts prefer less external stimulation.

The Innie-Outie preference is usually not an either/or; rather, it is a spectrum of preference. It's best to think of introversion and extroversion as a continuum, meaning that everybody has a little of both and nobody is 100 percent of anything all the time. Some people are very introverted or very extroverted and some people are only slightly introverted or extroverted. And some people are smack dab in the middle. (We call these people "ambiverts.") The key is to understand which preference you lean toward compared to which preference your boss leans toward.

For example, if your boss leans toward extroversion and you lean toward introversion, then your interactions and communication preferences may not be aligned. While in an ideal world your boss would modulate her behavior based on your preference, we know from research that most bosses only use one style of managing. That means chances are your extroverted or introverted boss will communicate and interact with you based on *their* preference, not *yours*. That's why it is essential for you to learn and adapt to *their* natural style of communication and energy sources.

Signs of the Innie and Outie Boss

While extroversion and introversion preferences aren't behaviors in and of themselves, they are *drivers* of behavior, and there are certain behaviors that are commonly associated with the preference. Review the following list. Which one seems to be more accurate of your boss, most of the time?

The Outie Boss: Leans Toward Extroversion	The Innie Boss: Leans Toward Introversion
■ Readily shares information	■ Shares minimal information
■ Sometimes over-shares information	■ Often under-shares information
■ Regularly has team meetings	■ Team meetings are infrequent
■ Talks a lot at team meetings	■ Listens more than talks at meetings
■ Can be long-winded	■ Can seem overly succinct or terse
■ Has an open-door policy (and means it)	■ Often works alone with door closed
■ Enjoys engaging with staff	■ Doesn't often shoot the breeze
■ Makes effort to get to know you	■ Does less relationship building
■ Feels warm and friendly	■ Feels a little closed off and aloof
■ Reveals his/her thought process	■ Reveals his/her thought process – only when asked
■ Always says hello	■ Forgets to say hello
■ Spends time walking about the office	■ Rarely walks around the office interacting
■ Checks in regularly	■ Check-ins are infrequent
■ Happy to talk face-to-face or on the phone	■ Prefers e-mail to face-to-face or phone
■ Likes to move to action quickly	■ Likes to reflect/process before taking action
■ Has a big network	
■ Enjoys meeting with people	■ Spends less time networking
■ Solicits opinions	■ Less apt to meet with people
■ Enjoys brainstorming with you or the team	■ Less likely to solicit opinions
■ Prone to thinking out loud	■ Not a huge fan of brainstorming
■ Responds quickly and frequently	■ Rarely thinks out loud
■ Doesn't mind interruptions	■ Slower at responding
■ Energy feels outward and expansive	■ Less open to interruptions
■ You generally know what they are thinking	■ Energy feels inward and contained
■ Works frequently with others	■ You rarely know what they are thinking
	■ Frequently works alone

Once you have determined whether your boss leans in or out, then take some time to reflect on and assess how well your preference is aligned with your boss's preference:

- Do you tend toward introversion or extroversion?
- In what ways are you the same or different from your boss?
- What do you want more of or less of from your boss?
- How are your respective introversion or extroversion preferences serving your needs?
- How are your respective introversion or extroversion preferences serving your boss's needs?
- What can you do differently, more of, less of to help *you* succeed with your boss?
- What can you do differently, more of, less of to help your *boss* succeed?

(If you don't know which is your preference, see the brief quiz at the end of this chapter.)

Some Examples of How This Dynamic May Show Up

I really enjoy working with my boss. He checks in regularly and never minds it when I pop in. We have great conversations, he is always ready to share information, and we usually know exactly what he thinks or wants. We have lots of team meetings where people are encouraged to share their ideas. Working with him is very energizing and engaging. (Assessment: An Outie working for an Outie.)

My boss can be a bit frustrating. I know she cares about us but I don't always feel that she is open and friendly. She never just pops over to say hello. I'm hesitant to interrupt her when she is in her office working because I get the sense that she might be annoyed. We have to ask a lot of questions because she isn't that good at sharing information. Sometimes it feels like pulling teeth. I wish we had more team meetings. I don't feel very connected to her. (Assessment: An Outie working for an Innie.)

My boss is really energetic and loves to talk about things. It's great *sometimes*, but I often feel drained by it. Meetings go on for too long and frequently feels like a waste of time. I feel myself getting impatient waiting for him to get to the point, and I wish that he would decide what he wants before he starts talking. I've recently started teleworking once a week, which has been wonderful. I'm able to get so much more done. I'm thinking of asking my boss if I can telework twice a week. (Assessment: An Innie working for an Outie.)

I love working for my boss. We are so sympatico on so many levels. Our office is calm, quiet, and peaceful. She leaves me alone and doesn't expect me to do a lot of socializing or chit-chatting. She tends to be very direct with what she wants and our meetings are brief and focused. She's very thoughtful about decisions and never acts rashly. The best part – we both love e-mail and texting. I love that she doesn't need a lot of face time with me. (Assessment: An Innie working for an Innie.)

Remember: there is nothing innately good or bad about either preference. Both are equally valuable aspects of the human condition. Both are essential to an effective workplace. The key is to find ways to *complement* and *harmonize* with each preference, not to *compete* or *clash* against it. If you are an Innie and your boss is an Outie you must learn their preference and adapt to it. If you are an Outie and your boss is an Innie, same thing. How do you do that? The next two chapters will provide plenty of ideas and strategies to manage up your Innie or Outie.

Quick and Dirty Extroversion-Introversion Quiz

Review each list. Circle the statements that **best describe you most of the time.** Don't overthink it. Just answer.

List A

1. I get energized from active involvement in events.
2. I enjoy being involved in lots of activities.

3. I enjoy group work and team projects.
4. Being around people energizes me.
5. I like to quickly move into action and make things happen.
6. I generally feel at home in the world.
7. I learn by talking things out and hearing from others.
8. People consider me "outgoing" or as a "people person."
9. I feel comfortable in groups.
10. I have a wide range of friends that I stay in contact with.
11. I enjoy external stimulation.
12. I prefer to work with others than work alone.
13. I don't mind being the center of attention.
14. I am the life of the party.
15. I get bored when I'm by myself.
16. I always feel comfortable around people.
17. I try not to keep in the background.
18. I tend to want others to pay attention to me.
19. I'm comfortable expressing my opinions; people generally know what I am thinking.
20. I'm a good communicator.
21. I am good with meeting new people.
22. I like to talk.
23. Disruptions at work don't bother me. I like the change of pace.
24. I like to try new things.
25. Call me! Let's talk!

List B

1. I get energized through spending time alone.
2. I prefer to focus on a small number of activities.
3. I prefer working on tasks alone where I can concentrate.
4. Being around too many people drains me.
5. I sometimes spend too much time reflecting and don't move into action quickly enough.
6. I often feel awkward or unsure of myself in new situations.
7. I learn best by thinking through things internally before talking about them.
8. I am seen as "reflective" or "reserved."

9. I feel more comfortable being alone than in groups.
10. I have a small group of friends that I prefer to spend time with.
11. Sometimes I like the idea of something better than the real thing.
12. I prefer to work alone.
13. I don't like to draw attention to myself.
14. Being around too many people drains me.
15. I rarely get bored being by myself.
16. I have to psych myself up to be around people.
17. I am comfortable being in the background.
18. I don't like too much attention from others.
19. I tend not to assert myself. I don't always let people know what I am thinking.
20. I'm a good listener.
21. I am quiet around strangers.
22. I don't talk a lot.
23. Disruptions at work really bother me; I like to stay focused.
24. I feel awkward around new people
25. E-mail me! I may not answer the phone.

If you circled more statements from the A list than the B list, chances are you lean toward extroversion. More B than A answers indicate a preference toward introversion. And if you have equal numbers of items circled from both lists then you might be an ambivert. Good for you; you can swing both ways.

3

The Innie

"In human intercourse the tragedy begins, not when there is misunderstanding about words, but when silence is not understood."

—Henry David Thoreau

Real-Life Story

Roger's list of complaints against his boss, Carol, was endless. "She doesn't communicate. She sits in her office with the door closed. We have no idea what she is thinking. She never walks around to see how we are doing. Getting information or feedback from her is like pulling teeth. She is not very friendly or warm and she certainly doesn't like being our boss. I mean, would it kill her to check in with us now and again? I really think she is a terrible manager." Roger had fallen into the trap of misinterpreting and judging Carol's introverted behaviors as bad management as opposed to understanding, adapting, and appreciating them as what they were – introverted preferences. What if, we asked Roger, her behavior is just an expression of introversion and not necessarily bad management? What if instead of reproving her

(continued)

21

(*continued*)

introverted needs and tendencies, you tried to adapt and align to them?

During the workshop, we helped Roger see that Carol had needs as an introvert that were different from his needs as an extrovert. And, while frustrating, there were proven ways in which Roger could approach and work with Carol to improve the relationship and help her be a better manager. Roger was game to try. He soon discovered that by being proactive about what he needed – scheduling more meetings, asking more questions, etc. – he was able to forge a better bond for himself and the team. But perhaps the most effective strategy that Roger used was letting go of his judgment and scorn. "Once I let go of being frustrated and judging her for what she 'should do' and how she 'should be,' I was able to be more empathetic, creative, and thoughtful in my dealings with her. I've even now come to appreciate some of her introverted qualities. Would I rather I didn't have to go the extra mile? Yes. Is it worth doing? Yes. I've learned a lot about working with introverts."

Introverted (Innie) Bosses can be great and they can be frustrating! The key is to understand it and work *with* the introversion and not *against* it. Working with an Introverted Boss means managing two important elements: communication style and energy style. You want to make sure you choose modes of communication that are effective for your Introverted Boss and that you interact with him in ways that maximize his energy and not drain it.

America is a very extroverted country and introverts are often misunderstood in the workplace. Their "contained" energy is often misunderstood and mislabeled as coldness, aloofness, or reticence. These labels are not very helpful as they create a story about your boss that may or may not be true. Instead it's important to understand that the introvert's source of energy and communication preferences may just be different from yours. Not better, not worse, just different!

Potential Benefits and Challenges of the Innie Boss

Some Potential Benefits of the Innie Boss:

They give you space
They tend to leave you alone and give you lots of personal space to get your work done.

They don't waste your time
Introverted Bosses usually don't initiate shooting-the-breeze type conversations, so your Innie Boss isn't likely to "waste your time" with idle chit-chat.

They think before they speak
Innies tend not to shoot from the hip, so when discussing work products and projects, their thoughts tend to be more complete and clear, especially if they've had time to process and think through their ideas.

They will listen to you
Introverts tend to spend more time listening than talking. Whether this makes them better listeners is up for debate – I mean, who knows what's going on inside their introverted heads? – but at least by the nature of their silence, you have a good at shot at getting air time!

Individuals who are more effusive, expressive, and extroverted may find the Introverted Boss frustrating or even uncomfortable to work with. Extroverts are looking (or wanting) the boss to offer up more – more chat, more supportive comments, more emotion, and more interaction. When these behaviors are missing or sparse, it can cause some people to read the boss as difficult or unfriendly. Not the stuff a good relationship is made of. At the same time, introverts also can find working with other introverts frustrating as well, especially if they feel too isolated from their boss. This challenge can be compounded, quite frankly, when introverted employees finds themselves too comfortable with the solitude to push past their preferences.

Some Potential Challenges (and Frustrations) of Working for an Innie Include:

Lack of information

Introverted Bosses aren't the best at information sharing. This means that you may not always have the information you need to succeed and the onus of getting that information is on you.

Lack of "friendliness"

An Introverted Boss may spend less time getting to know you personally. Building relationships with Innies takes time and energy – from you!

Closed-door appearance

Because introverts work best alone, they are probably not spending their time walking around and checking in. They may appear less available for spontaneous check-ins and you may worry about "bothering them" while they are working.

Less solicitous

Because Innies tend to process internally, they may also be less likely to solicit input on ideas and may not be big fans of "brainstorming." Decisions, plans, and strategic choices may come as a surprise to the team.

Proven Strategies to Manage Up the Introvert

1. **Take the initiative to meet.**
   One of the challenges of an introverted Boss is spending time with them. You will need to take the initiative on this. The best way to do this is to schedule one-on-one meetings in advance. Don't wait for your Innie to reach out to you. Get on the calendar.
2. **Give them time to process and prepare.**
   Tell them ahead of time what you want to talk about. Because introverts prefer to process information before speaking about it, they will appreciate the opportunity to prepare.
3. **Keep them in the loop.**
   Don't assume that because your Innie isn't initiating constant project check-ins with you that she is not interested in what is happening. She is. Make sure you keep your Innie

updated on your projects and endeavors. Either schedule brief project check-in meetings or calls, or send brief e-mail updates. This will help your boss keep a finger on the pulse of your department, appreciate your efforts, and stay apprised of your accomplishments.

4. **Limit impromptu "pop-in" meetings.**
   Instead of popping in every time you have a question, try instead to "bundle" your questions into one or two conversations a day.

5. **Embrace electronic communication.**
   Introverts generally respond well to e-mail, text, chat, etc. It allows them to both conserve personal energy and gather their thoughts in response. It's a two-fer!

6. **Don't be a chatterbox.**
   When meeting with your Innie, keep your conversation focused and concise. Too much chatter will quickly drain (and annoy) your Innie. Take a few minutes to gather and organize your thoughts before the meeting. It's also helpful to start your meetings with task talk rather than personal chit-chat.

Real-Life Story

Mary was the owner of several restaurants, which required her to split her time among them. One of her restaurants was managed by Sam, whom Mary described as a "raging extrovert." Mary found working with Sam draining and frustrating. "Quite frankly, I found him exhausting. He sapped my energy. It was impossible for me to call him up with a quick question or two because every conversation became a lengthy discussion. He loved to talk and wanted to tell me everything all the time. Honestly, I just didn't care. I didn't have the time or energy to listen to every story or his lengthy description of things. If I asked a simple question like 'What were the receipts last night?' instead of getting a simple answer, I got a play-by-play recap of the entire night. And when he needed my advice, he didn't stop talking long enough for me to formulate a thoughtful answer. It wore me out. I found myself avoiding calling him at all costs. I would go as long as possible

(continued)

> (*continued*)
>
> without connecting. I really liked Sam and he did a great job but I couldn't deal with his need for extroversion and connection. I know I was not the best boss that I could be. I'm also fairly confident that my lack of communication was equally as frustrating to him. It would have been useful for both of us to have had a conversation around introversion versus extroversion."

7. **Seek out other extroverts to "think out loud."**

    While introverts are perfectly capable of brainstorming and "thinking out loud," it isn't generally their preference. If you are an external processor, make sure you don't overdo this tendency with your Innie, as you may drain their patience. Instead, find another colleague to think out loud with. And if you do need to think out loud with your Innie, make sure you say that is what you are doing. You should literally say the words, "I'm just thinking out loud here..." I know it sounds simplistic, but it works. Trust me. I'm an Innie.

8. **Be okay with silence.**

    If you're talking to your Introverted Boss and he goes silent, do not make up a story about it. It doesn't mean he doesn't like what you're saying, and it also doesn't mean he loves what you're saying. It just means he is processing. Give your boss time to process and respond.

9. **Think W-A-I-T.**

    This stands for "Why am I talking?" One challenge for extroverts working for introverts is dealing with silence. Oftentimes, extroverts become uncomfortable with silence so they talk to fill the void. Resist this temptation. Introverts like and need silence. Remember, they like to process before responding. Try counting to eight before filling the space. You may be surprised by what develops.

10. **Ask questions.**

    Because introverts tend to introvert their thinking and decision making, they don't always do a great job of expressing their process or explaining themselves. Not getting enough information is one of the biggest challenges of working for an Innie Boss. It's not that introverts don't want to share, it's that it doesn't occur to them that you may need this information. So if you don't have the information or background that you need, you must take responsibility to ask questions. And when you ask questions, make them open-ended questions – things like "what, how, why, tell me about...." That will prompt them to give you more information.

11. **Invest in relationship building.**

    Don't assume because your Innie isn't outgoing and proactive with getting to know you that they don't want to have a relationship with you. They do. They just may go about it differently. Introverts tend to build relationships over time and in more one-on-one situations. To build a relationship with your Innie, look for opportunities to spend time together one-on-one. Suggest lunch or coffee. Find space at the end of meetings to learn more about your boss. Ask introverts questions about their experience. Listen to them without turning the conversation about yourself. Be patient with their ability to disclose and their pace of sharing. It may at first feel like pulling teeth, but if you sincerely invest time and energy, and are patient in your efforts, this investment will pay off.

12. **Respect their space.**

    Remember, introverts derive their energy from internal sources and are drained by too much external stimulation. This means that your Innie Boss needs alone time to recharge his or her batteries. Respect this need and provide this space. Pay attention to your boss's rhythms and try to work with them. Learn your boss's "prime time" for working and try to avoid bothering the Innie during that time. For example, if your Innie likes his or her alone time at the beginning and/or end of each day, then do what you can to respect this space and leave him or her alone at this time. Your boss will be forever grateful.

13. **Beware the Innie-Innie trap.**

    On the surface, an introvert who works with another introvert seems like it would be a match made in heaven. And in some ways, it is. Chances are you have a nice quiet, calm, and compatible working relationship. However, if this is your situation, please be aware of some potential pitfalls. Two intro-verts working together run the risk of behaving like two ships sailing past each other in the night. In other words, two introverts working together might not construct important connection points. If you are an Innie working for an Innie, please know that you can be more successful with your boss if you become more proactive about communication and relationship building. In other words, you might want to act more like an extrovert. This means you may have to get out of your comfort zone in order to make a conscious effort to connect. It will be harder for you because the Innie-Innie dynamic feels just so damn comfortable and easy! Take the time to schedule face-to-face meetings. Don't rely solely on e-mail. Have coffee with your boss. Speak up. Put on your extrovert pants and build the relationship!

Real-Life Story

After having worked for plenty of extroverts, Willa was excited to work for an introvert like herself. "Finally," she thought, "peace and quiet! I'll have plenty of time to get my work done without expending unnecessary energy with all that talky-talk stuff." It wasn't long, however, before Willa realized that neither she nor her boss, Abe, were making a meaningful connection beyond the passing off of tasks. They would go days without talking, communicating mostly through texts and e-mail. While it was a pleasant and easy-going relationship, Willa soon realized that she found herself wanting and needing more. All too often she was guessing at what Abe wanted and was starting to feel out of the loop on projects and strategic directions. She also began to question whether or not her work was hitting the mark, as Abe wasn't very forthright with feedback other than "great job" and "thanks." Willa decided that if she wanted more from Abe, she was going to have to ask for it. She started requesting short meetings, mixing them up between talking in person and telephone calls. She took the initiative and it paid off. "Honestly, it wasn't that hard once I forced myself out of my comfort zone. Abe was very receptive to our meetings and was very forthright in providing information and feedback, once I asked. I was careful to always give him the topics ahead of time and I tried hard to be efficient with his time. We even now have a regular monthly coffee; of course I have to schedule them, but taking the initiative has been a game changer for me and our working relationship. I am a thousand times more connected and in the loop than before."

Strategy Recap

- Schedule meetings and be proactive in connecting and relationship building with your Innie.
- Tell your boss ahead of time what you want to discuss.
- Don't overwhelm with too many "pop-ins."
- Ask open-ended questions.
- Give your Innie space to process.
- Don't make up stories about your boss's silence.
- Use e-mail, text, or chat.
- Don't be a chatterbox.
- Understand the Innie's need for a little solitude and alone time.
- Overcome your own introversion to avoid the Innie-Innie hurdle.

4

The Outie

"It was impossible to get a conversation going, everybody was talking too much."

—Yogi Berra

Real-Life Story

Tim, who works in the medical supply industry, thought his boss, Carl, was cray-cray. And flaky. And unfocused. Carl just talked way too much. To make matters worse, Carl would often contradict himself midsentence. Tim found himself confused, impatient, and frustrated. He had a hard time understanding what Carl wanted and began to resent the time that Carl wasted every day prattling on and on. But the part that really bothered Tim was that he couldn't get a word in edgewise. Carl never paused long enough for Tim to contribute, and by the time he did pause Tim was checked out. It was all he could do not to scream, "Shut up, already!" whenever Carl got on a tear.

Does this sound familiar? If so, you are probably working for an extrovert. And if you are an introvert who works for an extreme extrovert, this story may have sent a shiver down your spine. Tim's challenge was that he was an introvert trying to work for an extreme extrovert. For Tim, the experience was grueling and arduous.

The Extrovert (Outie) Boss can be both a blessing and a curse. She is talkative and readily shares information. He enjoys team meetings and likes to have brainstorming sessions. She has a proclivity to move into action very quickly. He asks you about your weekend and readily tells you about his. An extrovert's door is often open and he or she enjoys discussing projects and ideas out loud. Extroverted leaders prize communication, openness, and group work. They get their energy through socialization and interaction. But they can also be exhausting and draining if their extroversion is too high or yours is too low.

The good news is that working for an extrovert is fairly straight-forward. Because the nature of management requires communication and interaction with team members, many extroverts are naturally well suited to be successful with those elements of leading. In fact, studies show that while the general US population is evenly split between introverts and extroverts, the majority of managers and leaders type as extroverts.

Potential Benefits and Challenges of the Outie Boss

Some Benefits of the Outie Boss Include:

They enjoy engaging you
Because extroverts get their energy from external stimuli, they usually enjoy engaging with their people and do so on a regular basis. Relationship building tends to be important to Outie Bosses. They tend to be responsive, friendly, and inviting.

You know where they stand
Outies tend to readily share information. They will extrovert both their opinions and their thought processes. If you talk to your Outie about a project for ten minutes and you don't know where she stands, then you haven't listened!

They have active networks
Extroverts tend to collect people, and their networks are substantial both inside and outside the organization. This can help you and your team accomplish your goals.

They are action oriented
Multiple studies show that extroverts are energized by taking action and enjoy making things happen for themselves, the organization, and the team.

Challenges of working for the Outie come into play when there is either too much extroversion (aka the "raging extrovert") or when introverts don't understand the nature of their Outie Boss.

Some Potential Challenges (and Frustrations) of Working for an Outie Include:

Thoughts may seem unclear or confusing
Outies tend to be external information processors and therefore have a penchant for thinking out loud. This can be confusing for others who don't understand it and annoying for people who prefer internal processing.

May spend too much time talking
This can show up as too much detail, too much social chit-chat, too much brainstorming, or just too much explaining. It also shows up as not enough listening.

Too much information, too soon
Sometimes the Outie Boss will over-share information or share information prematurely.

May move too quickly to action
Outies' preference for action puts them at risk for jumping into action too quickly without allowing enough time for reflection.

May be draining
High levels of extroversion from the boss can be physically, cognitively, and emotionally draining for the team, even for other extroverts.

Proven Strategies to Manage Up the Extrovert

1. **Listen to them talk.**
   Outie Bosses like to share and usually have a need to be heard. Listen to them. Show interest in their ideas and thoughts. Help

them sort out their ideas. Exhibit enthusiasm and active listening skills. Time consuming? Yes. Worthwhile? Definitely.

2. **Exhibit friendliness.**

   Social niceties go a long way with Outies. Smile. Say hello. Invite them for coffee, lunch, etc. Attend team events. Demonstrate your interest in relationship building. Use open body language when communicating. If you are an introvert, be prepared to share a little and save a little.

3. **Don't take everything as gospel.**

   Extroverts tend to process out loud, think out loud. Introverts tend not to do that. If you're working for an Extrovert Boss, be aware that everything Outies say may not be actionable. They may just need to get it out. It can be confusing as you try to follow their thinking process. Sit tight, the storm will pass.

4. **Clarify and recap.**

   When your Outie Boss is thinking out loud it can be helpful to clarify and recap to make sure you are both on the same page. At the end of a meeting with an extrovert, recap the conversation, salient points, and action items. Say something like, "Okay, let me recap what I think our next steps are . . . is that right?" You might be surprised at what you think you heard and what your boss actually meant. This will save you a ton of time and will help you avoid wasted effort.

Real-Life Story

Bob is a self-described extrovert who learned the hard way that his Outie preference sometimes confused his team. "One of the biggest lessons I learned as a new leader was that my team took everything I said at face value. In meetings, I enjoyed thinking out loud and would say things like, 'We should do this, or we should consider that, or what if we went in this direction?' To me these statements were simply thoughts for discussion and consideration. I didn't mean them literally. So, imagine my surprise when, six months later, my staff would come and say to me, here's that thing you wanted. Of course, I had no idea what they were talking about. I had totally forgotten that I had even said those things. Finally, after months of confusion and false starts one of my braver employees spoke up about this dynamic. Once this blind spot of mine was illuminated, the team learned to manage my out-loud thinking tendencies by clarifying and confirming decisions and projects before moving forward. Their willingness to manage me up has helped me be a better leader!"

5. **Speak up!**

   Don't be a wallflower with your Outie Boss. Speak up. Share ideas and thoughts. Extroverts don't expect your thoughts to be perfect; they just want to hear them. This can be hard for introverts who prefer to process first. Get comfortable jumping into the discussion. The Outie Boss welcomes communication and banter. Besides, if you wait too long to give your opinion, you may lose the opportunity to add value.

6. **Get face time.**

   Make the effort to physically *talk* with your Outie Boss. Don't over-rely on e-mail, chat, or text. Take the time to see your boss in person or pick up the phone to speak with him or her. External interactions are important to extroverts, because they'll get more energy from you. If your Outie feels energized by you, that's going to help your relationship.

7. **Explain your silence.**

   Silence is hard for many extroverts. And, like many people, they will make up a story about it. If you are an internal processor and need to go silent to reflect before answering, be prepared to tell your Outie Boss that you need a moment to process. Literally say the words, "Give me a moment to process."

8. **Recharge when you can.**

   Introverts working for extroverts can find the experience very draining. Make sure you build recharge time into your workday when and where you can. Your energy matters!

9. **Check in regularly and don't ghost.**

   Even if you are a highly independent self-starter, make sure you stay in communication with your Extrovert Boss. Check in regularly and make your presence, commitment, and accomplishments known. Extroverts are highly attuned to the external environment. Make sure your boss is aware you are there!

10. **Welcome brainstorming.**

    Extroverts have a tendency for external processing; therefore, they tend to enjoy a good brainstorming session. In fact, the very nature of the brainstorm is about extroversion. Learn to love and participate in these sessions even if you don't believe in them.

11. **Manage the Outie-Outie dynamic.**

    Extroverts often enjoy working for other extroverts. The Outie-Outie combination can produce an energetic, satisfying, and action-filled partnership. However, too much extroversion on both sides can also create problems with task clarity and time-management. Here are a couple of tips for Outies working for other Outies:

    o Manage the social chatting. Extroverts with extroverts can spend a lot of time on social chatting. This is great, until you start feeling trapped by so much chatting with your boss and it gets in the way of your work.

    o Control tangents. Take responsibility for refocusing conversations when necessary. If you find yourself or your Outie Boss going off on yet another tangent, it's okay to rein it back in. Simply say something like, "Hey Debbie, I think we've strayed. You/we/I were talking about X. Is it okay if we go back to that? I still have some questions/thoughts …"

    o Beware of hijacking the conversation. Hijacking occurs when one person takes control of the conversation and makes it about something else. Hijacking leads to tangents. People hate to be hijacked.

Real-Life Story

Josie is a public affairs specialist for a large public utility company. She and her boss, Melanie, are both extroverts. At first Josie was in heaven. She and Melanie quickly established a friendly rapport and a lively, productive relationship. Josie felt well supported and was able to quickly learn her job and earn Melanie's trust. The problem is that now their combined extroversion was getting in the way of Josie's productivity. In the beginning, Josie's extended interactions with her boss were helpful and energizing, but now these exchanges felt taxing and time-consuming. She didn't want to hurt Melanie's feelings or damage their relationships, she just wanted (and needed) a little more space, a little less conversation.

In order to solve this challenge, Josie had to first consider her own contributions to the problem. Josie sincerely loved interacting with Melanie and she found herself totally engaged in extraneous conversation. Josie had a habit of popping in to Melanie's office every time she had a question, and, like many Extrovert Bosses, Melanie embraced an open-door policy that encouraged this behavior. Josie admitted that she was "addicted" to the immediacy of the problem solving. Once Josie realized that she was part of the problem, she understood that she could be part of the solution. Instead of popping in every time she had a question, Josie would save up questions for one meeting, or she would shoot Melanie a quick e-mail or text.

Josie also started timing her pop-ins for times when Melanie's calendar indicated an upcoming meeting. This helped Josie and Melanie limit the length of these pop-in conversations to ten to fifteen minutes. Josie also paid attention to Melanie's event calendar. If Josie knew Melanie had an industry lunch to attend, Josie would plan her day accordingly – trying to get as much work done as possible before Melanie returned – as Melanie always enjoyed engaging in a lengthy post-event debrief with Josie. Sometimes this meant eating lunch at her desk or coming in a little bit early on occasion. Josie's final strategy was to schedule their regular check-in meetings for late in the day, an hour or so before she knew Melanie had to leave for school pick-up. Josie found her strategies worked like a charm. She was able to maintain her robust relationship with Melanie while gaining enough control over her schedule so that she was able to regain productivity. All it took was a little strategizing and adapting. She wasn't so much stopping Melanie's extroverting as she was planning for it and managing it as effectively as possible.

Strategy Recap

- Engage the Outie in conversation.
- Exhibit friendliness and openness.
- Speak up!
- Listen to your boss's ideas and help her sort out external processing.
- Recap action items before taking action.
- Make time for face-to-face conversations or pick up the phone and talk to your boss.
- Welcome and participate in brainstorming.
- Manage your own extroversion to avoid the Outie-Outie trap.

5

Workplace Styles – Assessing Your Boss's Workstyle Personality

*"Treat others as **they** would like to be treated."*

—The platinum Rule

The golden rule says we should treat others as we would like to be treated. This works great when we all want to be treated the same – meaning we all want and value the same type of interaction. But in the real world, especially in the workplace, people have different wants and needs and different ways of expressing those wants and needs. Some people prefer to think fast, talk fast, and act fast, while others prefer to take a more moderate, measured, and careful approach to work and communication. Some people are social and friendly at work and they like to build relationships and get to know their colleagues, while others exhibit less friendliness and may value relationships primarily as a vehicle to accomplish tasks. Some people are very assertive and direct about their opinions, wants, and needs while others are less assertive and more accommodating and solicitous of other's ideas, opinions, needs, and wants. Some folks are impatient for results, others very patient. Some need tons of data to make decisions, while others may need little or no data. Some are very emotive and expressive, while others are more emotionally reserved and contained. And the list goes on. The key here is to understand the similarities and differences between you and your boss so that you can adapt your behavior accordingly. You want to treat your boss how *he or she* likes to be treated, not necessarily how *you* like to be treated. This is about your boss, not you.

Four Common Workstyle Personalities: A Simple Model for Understanding Your Boss

To manage up effectively, it's helpful to consider your boss's workstyle personality. Workstyle personality refers to the types of behaviors people tend to use when interacting with others at work. Think of it as one's operating system: It is the way we react to and interact with the outside world. While nobody is 100 percent of anything all the time, most of us tend to exhibit fairly consistent traits and behaviors in our dealings with others. These traits, behaviors, and preferences are what make up our workstyle personality. Understanding both the differences and similarities in your workstyle personality compared to your boss's is a practical and effective way to begin to manage up.

These four styles are basic workstyle personalities. See if you can identify which one (or ones) best describe you and your boss.

The Advancer

Advancers are highly focused on task, achieving results, and taking action. They are usually less concerned with building warm and fuzzy relationships. They are often perceived as confident, work oriented, efficient, and demanding. They can also be seen as dominating, harsh, and cold. They are direct in their communication, sometimes even brusque. They are goal oriented and can be impatient with others who cannot keep up or take too long to make decisions or take action. They are fast decision makers and pragmatic in their approach. They seek control of their environments and are energized by overcoming obstacles, winning, and accomplishing goals. For the Advancer, everything is about advancing task and getting results as efficiently and quickly as possible. Advancers respect competency, action, and results. And they love to be in charge. Characteristics of the Advancer include:

- Fast paced, bordering on impatient.
- Leads from the head. Focuses on tasks over people.
- Seeks control and being in charge. Readily takes authority.
- Confident and assertive in their opinions and decisions.
- Strong willed and emotionally controlled.
- Decisive and pragmatic. Makes quick decisions based on available and relevant data.
- Fast acting and quick to move from planning to action (abhors analysis paralysis).
- Straightforward, to the point, and direct in communication.
- Takes risk and seeks challenges.
- Dislikes inaction, indecision, and inefficiency.
- Prefers maximum freedom to decide and act.
- Low tolerance for other people's feelings and advice.
- Works quickly and independently.
- Competitive and likes to win.
- Can be impatient and insensitive.
- When stressed may grab control, be overly critical, or become autocratic.

Positive traits:
Strong, decisive, determined, pragmatic, efficient, objective, businesslike.

Potential negative traits:
Aggressive, dictatorial, arrogant, insensitive, unbending, dominating, impatient.

The Energizer

Energizers are full of energy, personality, and optimism. They are the ultimate "people" people. They are sociable, stimulating, enthusiastic, and good at involving and motivating others. They are known for their enthusiasm, humor, and risk taking. They are adept at selling their ideas to others. They are often perceived by others as persuasive, high-energy, creative, and impulsive. Energizers are idea oriented and have little tolerance for routine. They are happiest when focused on future ideas and plans. They are quick (sometimes too quick) to react and they are quite comfortable expressing both their ideas and their feelings. They react quickly and often seem to make decisions based on opinions or intuition. They love to start new projects but may lose interest in the details or in completing projects. Additional characteristics of the Energizer include:

- Fast paced and energetic.
- Leads from the heart. Focuses on people and relationships.
- Outgoing and enthusiastic and usually interacts well with others at work.
- Makes spontaneous actions and decisions and may jump from one activity to another.
- Good at persuading and motivating others.
- Fears being ignored or rejected.
- Likes to be acknowledged publicly and often seeks the spotlight.
- Dislikes routine and complexity and can get annoyed with too many details.
- Tends to generalize and exaggerate.
- Achieves goals when motivated, challenged, and excited.
- Likes involvement and dislikes being alone.
- Often uses intuition or "gut" to make decisions.
- Creative and future focused, always thinking about a new way.
- Fast acting; ready to jump on a new project with limited need to plan.
- More interested in starting projects than finishing them.
- Wants others to be excited about his or her ideas and loves to "sell" the latest idea to others.
- When stressed may get sarcastic and unkind.

Positive traits:
Enthusiastic, imaginative, extroverted, persuasive, spontaneous, active.

Potential negative traits:
Superficial, immature, overbearing, impulsive, manipulative, unrealistic, undisciplined.

The Evaluator

Evaluators prize quality, precision, and accuracy. They tend to be organized and want all the facts (and history) before taking action or making a decision. Their preferred approach is to minimize risk by looking at all the options before making a decision. They are the quintessential "measure twice, cut once" type. They value correctness, precision, prudence, and objectivity. They are methodical and process oriented. They conform to standard operating procedures, organizational rules, and historical ways of doing things (usually because they wrote the procedures). They typically have slower reaction times and work more carefully than other types. They are perceived as serious, industrious, persistent, and exacting. They respect data and may come across as critical or picky. They are prone to perfectionism. Characteristics of the Evaluator include:

- Moderate paced and task oriented.
- Leads from the head. Focuses on tasks more than people.
- Thoughtful, careful, fact oriented, and precise.
- Seeks perfection, quality, and accuracy in everything; if it's worth doing, it's worth doing right.
- Cautious decision maker. Seeks minimum risk through maximum information.
- Methodical and process oriented.
- Needs things done right and may overthink things.
- Relies on thorough data collection. Prone to analysis paralysis.
- Steadfast, deliberate, and unemotional.
- Likes, promotes, and adheres to systematic approaches, structures, and processes.
- Dislikes personal involvement or emotional situations.
- Works slowly and precisely.
- Values correctness, accuracy, stability, and predictable outcomes.
- Good at objective evaluation and problem solving.

- Avoids group work, preferring to work alone.
- Can be seen as overcritical and unresponsive.
- When stressed may withdraw or become headstrong.

Positive traits:
Detailed, factual, logical, systematic, precise, questioning, quality oriented.

Potential negative traits:
Critical, negative, dogmatic, nitpicking, isolated, inflexible.

The Harmonizer

Harmonizers value people, relationships, stability, and harmony. For harmonizers, the workplace climate is very important. They want to help people be successful and happy. Harmonizers value personal relationships, helping others, and being liked. Their favored approach is to get consensus and to mediate between disparate opinions because they believe that the best solution is one where everyone is "on board." They specialize in compassion, loyalty, compromise, and building trust. Others tend to perceive them as kind, good with people, and somewhat self-effacing. Harmonizers are super cooperative and will often sacrifice their own time to help others. They value teamwork and team building. They are careful decision makers, often preferring to solicit the ideas and opinions of others before moving into actions or making decisions. They care about quality work and don't respond well to constant pressure or "fire drills." Their preference for stability and harmony can cause them to appear to be hesitant to change. Typically, they are friendly, supportive, respectful, willing, dependable, and agreeable and they respect others who model those traits. Additional characteristics of the Harmonizer:

- Moderate paced and relationship oriented.
- Leads from the heart. Focuses on people's well-being.
- Friendly and relates well to others.
- Open, receptive, supportive to ideas, wants, and needs of others.
- Likes to build close, personal relationships.
- Enjoys and promotes teamwork.
- Dislikes interpersonal conflict.

- Actively listens to others and often enjoys counseling others.
- Cooperative, amiable, and willing to help others.
- Works hard to gain support of others.
- Slow at taking new action or making decisions.
- Dislikes risk taking and may be uncomfortable and hesitant with change and uncertainty.
- Values and respects organizational hierarchy.
- Seeks stability, organization, and predictable routines.
- Wants to be respected, liked, and approved of.
- May be uncomfortable telling others what to do.
- When stressed may become indecisive and submissive.

Positive traits:
Friendly, cooperative, loyal, diplomatic, understanding, helpful, agreeable.

Potential negative traits:
Soft, indecisive, gullible, too laid-back, cowardly, weak.

Mono or Combo

Most people's reaction when considering these four styles is to say that they fit into more than one profile, which is absolutely right! People are rarely ever just one thing. However, most people do tend toward one dominant style. In addition, many people exhibit a strong secondary style. It is not uncommon for an Advancer to also incorporate some of the qualities of the Energizer or the Evaluator. The key is to identify your and your boss's most used dominant style or styles and find ways to assimilate and compliment those styles.

> **Remember**
>
> The key objective of the workstyle personality concept is to understand your own style, identify and understand the style of your boss, and then adapt so that you can interact with your boss the way he or she prefers. It's the platinum rule: treat others as *they* want to be treated. The following chapters will explore how to navigate and succeed with each of these workstyle personalities.

6

The Energizer

"You can't expect to hit the jackpot if you don't put a few nickels in the machine."

—Flip Wilson

Real-Life Story

Benjie was so excited when Don hired him to be his chief of staff. Benjie had worked with Don at a prior company and had thoroughly enjoyed the experience. Don was a dynamic, fast-paced person with big ideas and the courage to take risks. There was never a dull moment working with Don. There were always lots of exciting new projects and room to try new things. But best of all, Don was fun. He was always upbeat and had a way of making everyone smile. Plus, he always had your back and was always there to support and encourage. But when Benjie arrived at his new job he was dismayed to see the team was a mess. Things were disorganized and chaotic. The staff was floundering and running around like chickens with their heads cut off. It was clearly evident to Benjie that there was a huge chasm between the team and Don's leadership style. Benjie knew he had walked into a mess, a mess that he had to clean up.

The Energizer Boss

Fun, inspiring, and enthusiastic. And, yes, sometimes exasperating. Energizers are people focused, inviting, fast paced, and enthusiastic. Their door is always open and every idea is worth exploring. Energizers have a lot of energy and they want to use that energy to support the team. If they're not moving, changing, or trying something new, the Energizer gets bored. An Energizer Boss is a dream come true for energetic employees who also thrive in a fast-paced environment, but they can be overwhelming for others due to their lack of follow-through to see projects to completion.

Discover the Drivers: Understanding the Energizer Boss

It's all about people

Energizer Bosses are people focused and move at a fast pace. They love getting things done by motivating others and working with other people. They prefer a conversation-based approach to completing work and can quickly lose momentum when they must spend long periods of time working independently. Energizers don't care too much for formal roles and responsibilities. They prefer a flatter organizational structure and are generally very approachable.

Bored by routine

Energizer Bosses are open to trying new ideas and frequently willing to test things out, and they like to live in the world of possibilities and ideas. They like to see the big picture of ideas and don't have a lot of interest in details. Routine approaches to work bore them. Their least favorite phrase is, "This is how we've always done it."

Desire to help others

Energizer Bosses want everyone to succeed. They are there to provide coaching, encouragement, and support. Energizers are champions for change and love motivating the team. You may notice they tend to stand at meetings because they just have too much enthusiasm to contain by sitting behind a table. Their hands do as much talking as their mouth.

Fast ideas and fast action

Energizer Bosses may jump on board with a new idea before you think it's been well thought through. After some high-level discussion, they feel that the best way to know if an idea is going to work is to just do it. They trust their gut to decide if an idea is worth exploring. They are willing to take risks and see more value in "failing fast" and trying again than by slow, cautious, and fussy action.

Energized by starting (more than finishing)

Energizer Bosses have a lot of energy and enthusiasm for starting new projects and implementing new ideas. The beginning of a project is fun and exciting. Once it's time to drill down into the details to execute and maintain a project, an Energizer Boss will likely excuse herself and allow others to step up. Energizers will get behind almost any idea with full support, but their interest quickly fizzles when it comes to details and timelines. By the time you are done with the planning phase, they have already moved on to the next thing.

Loves brainstorming

Energizer Bosses believe that two heads are better than one (and that five heads are even better) and that ideas are better formulated out loud than in silence. They're apt to invite the team to bounce ideas around and probably love sticky notes, flipcharts, and markers more than you think is appropriate for an adult. Inviting the team to share ideas is a key component of team building and gaining buy-in on projects and decisions. They want you to have a voice.

Social hour (every hour, on the hour)

Often exuberant and outgoing, Energizers love to get to know the team. They want to check in on work-based conversations, but they also want to get to know you as a person. They love building coalitions, teams, and movements. For the Energizer, work is only as good as the people involved. Relationships matter.

Energizer Bosses are generally very friendly and care about people. They usually have an open door so you can check in easily and you don't have to worry about being a disruption. They are okay with you making mistakes, as long as you are willing to admit them, and will help you to correct the problem. Energizer Bosses truly care about you as a person and want you to be yourself at work. They thrive on helping team members succeed. They love focusing on the future and encourage team members to generate new ideas and use creative problem solving. Another great benefit of Energizers is the ability to tap into their network. Because Energizers value people and relationships, they often have extensive networks of friends and colleagues, and they are usually more than happy to make connections for people they care about.

On the downside, the Energizer Boss might spend more time on seemingly social conversations than you feel you have time for. These conversations can cause stress if you feel you can't get away and that you have a lot of work waiting for you at your desk. Their willingness to jump at new ideas may seem poorly thought through and a bad use of resources. You may feel imposed upon or confused by their new ideas and your role in executing them. Their priorities can shift on a dime and once they start a project, they may lose interest in completing it. In short, the Energizer may at times seem flaky and disorganized.

Proven Strategies to Manage Up the Energizer Boss

1. **Build the relationship.**
   Energizer Bosses are people focused. Their currency in the workplace is relationships, so take the time to build one. Energizers truly believe that they will be better leaders to you if they can establish a relationship with you and know you on a personal level. Taking time for conversations and relationship building leads to more effective and efficient work relationships in the long run with this boss. It's time consuming, but worth it.

2. **Think fast, move fast.**
   Energizers are fast moving and fast talking. Try your best to keep up. Be prepared to have plenty of brainstorming and blue-sky conversations. They don't expect perfection on the first round (or sometimes even the second). They are often willing to "fail fast" and learn from their mistakes rather than miss an opportunity to make a novel impact because of overanalysis or extreme cautiousness. Get comfortable with change, be flexible in execution, and above all join in the fun.

3. **Get excited!**
   The Energizer Boss does not want to go it alone with ideas. Get energized around the ideas and point out the best parts. Look for something that you can get excited about, even if you don't agree

with it overall. There will be time to disagree, but wait until after the initial discussion. It is likely that your boss will soon be moving on to something else, so don't waste capital pointing out the flaws in an idea that will probably get dropped anyway.

4. **Listen up!**

Energizers are full of ideas, thoughts, opinions, and dreams. Some of them are even good ones. Because Energizers value relationships, they value interpersonal communication and, above all, being heard. It can be time consuming, but Energizers tend to trust people who take the time to listen to them. You don't have to agree with them, but if they feel truly heard, they will feel valued. If they feel valued, they will trust you. So, next time your Energizer wants to wax poetic about a new idea, throw her a bone and hear her out.

5. **Don't be an Eeyore.**

If you are always pointing out the problems with ideas right off the bat, the Energizer Boss will quickly get frustrated with you. Nothing bums out an Energizer more than a wet blanket or whiner. No Debbie Downers allowed. Even when faced with tough projects, try to be upbeat and optimistic. Your boss needs positive energy from people throughout the work day. You will have more support for your ideas and will be viewed more favorably if you project some enthusiasm.

6. **Plan and execute.**

The Energizer Boss loves nothing more than people who can take ideas off his plate and bring them to fruition. The person who can take ideas, put a plan in place, and execute that plan is the perfect yin to his yang. Together, you will get a lot done and he will really appreciate your contributions to the team. **Bonus:** The Energizer Boss likes to give credit where credit is due. You will be recognized for your efforts.

7. **Double-check ideas.**

Don't assume that every idea that comes out of your Energizer Boss's mouth is an action item. She loves to brainstorm and shoot ideas, even if there is no intention of executing the idea. Don't hesitate to ask for clarification so that you focus your energy on the right things. Take notes at team meetings or when your boss drops by your office, and then follow up later to ask for guidance on priorities.

8. **Show your face.**

   The Energizer Boss likes to see people. He wants you to volunteer for focus groups, brainstorming sessions, and other team meetings. Doing work face-to-face will give you the opportunity to build a relationship with your boss, which will serve you well in the long run. Schedule weekly meetings with him to share ideas, review current projects, and continue to build your relationship.

9. **Master the art of the pop-in.**

   Energizers love the pop-in. While their open-door policy is great for access and quick conversations, it can also lead to extensive conversations that you may not be in the mood for. If you just need a quick word, try to pop in with your head only, leaving your body outside the office or cubicle. Have an escape plan. Something like, "Hey boss, I'm about to get on a conference call, and just needed to get a quick answer to XYZ."

10. **Be creative.**

    The Energizer Boss wants you to bring ideas and solutions, not problems. Stay on the lookout for potential areas for improvement, come up with a few possible ways to move forward, and then bring those ideas to the table. The Energizer Boss may love new ideas, but she doesn't want them to all be her own.

11. **Praise them publicly.**

    Because Energizers are innately social beings, they respond to appreciation and authentic praise. All the better if the praise happens in public. **Key word here:** authentic.

Real-Life Story

In order to make this situation work for everybody, Benjie decided he needed a two-pronged approach. One prong was to help Don understand the context of his leadership. Don had replaced a manager who was his exact opposite – a careful, cautious, low-key perfectionist. Therefore, working for Don felt like whiplash to the team; they just didn't know how to deal with him. Benjie helped Don see that he would be better served by slowing it down a bit until the team started to understand Don's style. The second prong was to help the team develop strategies to work better with Don.

"I helped the team understand and hopefully appreciate Don's style. I explained that Don thrives on exploring new ideas and that it was best to hear him out before pointing out all the reasons why his idea wouldn't work. I encouraged them to listen for elements of the idea that they could incorporate. The team also had to learn that Don didn't expect perfection. In fact, he was willing to accept mistakes as long as we learned from them. I told them that Don was an innovator and that this was an opportunity for them to try new things. I also needed them to know that just because Don liked to have fun at work didn't mean he doesn't take things seriously – he does. I also explained to them that Don tends to focus on the big picture and doesn't like to be bogged down with execution details – that's our job. I helped them understand that when they were confused about priorities they needed to be proactive and ask Don. And last, I suggested that if they wanted to be successful with Don, they needed to get comfortable with change. The staff who were able to pivot and adapt to Don's style did very well on our team."

Strategy Recap

- Be positive and support new ideas from the outset.
- Get involved in team projects and volunteer to lead.
- Keep track of new projects, but follow up before spending time on plans and details.
- Meet with your boss regularly and get to know her as a person.
- Seek guidance for priorities and then execute the details.

7

The Advancer

"I never worry about action, but only about inaction."

—Winston Churchill

Real-Life Story

Veronica is the chief operating officer of an animal welfare organization. Her boss, Heather, is a smart, energetic, hard-driving, no-nonsense, just-get-it-done kind of a person. "Working for Heather is complicated and fascinating. I've never worked for anyone quite like her. On the one hand, she is this amazing CEO. She has a really clear and ambitious vision for the organization and drives hard to accomplish that vision. She is strong, courageous, and decisive. She has pushed us to take risks and has expanded the scope of our services dramatically. She has made the organization very successful; in fact, we've flourished.

"On the other hand, Heather is the most difficult person for whom I've ever worked. She drives us hard all the time. When I first started, she said to me: 'I know you can do more than you think you can do, and I'm going to push you and there are times when I'm going to tell you to do stuff that you don't want to do,

(continued)

55

(continued)

you don't think you can do, but I'm going to make you do it.' I've never worked for someone with whom I didn't have some sort of personal connection, but Heather made it clear that we were not going to be friends. In fact, she literally said to me early on, 'We are not friends.' So, okay, I'm fine with not being friends, I just wish she had a little more sensitivity to others. She comes across as very self-centered and doesn't take time to consider other people. Everyone is at her disposal. If she wants to meet with you, there is never a 'Are you free at such and such a time?' Instead she tells us when she wants to meet and then everyone is expected to rearrange their schedules around her. Heather acts like a Queen Bee who expects everyone to mold themselves to her.

"Some days I want to canonize her and some days I want to shoot her out of a cannon."

Veronica works for an Advancer. And Advancers like to advance – fast. Advancer Bosses are results oriented, driven, decisive, ambitious, and confident. They focus on task, task, task. They rarely focus on people and often exhibit little concern for workplace relationships. They are often seen as dominating. They are usually very direct in their communication and tend to be impatient for progress. They are natural competitors who love a good challenge and are very open to taking risks. Some people love working for them, others find them a tough pill to swallow. I should know – I am one.

Discover the Drivers: Understanding the Advancer Boss

Results over relationships

Advancers are fast paced and focused on results. They value what you can produce and contribute to the team, but not so much who you are as a person or what your emotional needs at work might be. They do not need or want to know how you feel and are not impressed by what you intend to do in your position. Advancers want to see results and to see them quickly. They aren't impressed by excuses or neediness in employees. They work by continually moving the ball forward and they appreciate those who speed up the process. Employees who are slow, methodical, and ask a lot of questions can frustrate an Advancer Boss.

Need for speed

If you have an Advancer Boss, you will notice that they are almost always moving – literally. They talk fast, they move quickly from one thing to another, and they rarely sit still in their office. Advancers are action oriented and use their time to get things done; well, started at least. Advancers like to hit the ground running on new, exciting things and then delegate the details to others. They want projects to be finished, but they are usually too busy moving on to the next thing to be involved in completing the project. They work well with those who can take care of the details but who don't slow down the process.

Need to succeed

Advancers seek success. They thrive on competition, winning, getting results, and overcoming challenges. Frequently, Advancers seek traditional notions of success – power, status, and prosperity – either for themselves, their team, or their organization, and they value those who do the same. Advancers will typically monitor progress and results using these types of benchmarks. They want to know how sales compare to last quarter and will be most on board with projects that bring in more money, new clients, etc. It's not that Advancers don't care about relationships or employee satisfaction, but those are not their main motivators. In addition, it is not all about personal pride or greed. They genuinely want to see the business do well and they thrive on the challenge of setting bigger goals.

Craves control

An Advancer's inner drive for success is often manifested by an outer expression of control and therefore they may come across as bossy or domineering. Simply put, Advancers have confidence in their vision and enjoy steering the ship. To them, it is more efficient to "tell" rather than "ask." Advancers will occasionally show interest in your ideas, but at the end of the day, they often put their ideas first and will expect you to prioritize accordingly. For some, this can feel like stifling creativity, while others are perfectly happy to follow suit.

Hates hand-holding

Advancers value independence in themselves and others. While Advancers love being in control, they are not usually micromanagers. They are interested in the *what*, not the *how*. So, they will not meddle in how you complete a task, but they will be completely absorbed in what tasks are on your to-do list and, more importantly, your accomplishments. Advancers are usually involved in the beginning and end of projects, but care less about the middle bits. The sooner you get started and the sooner you get it done, the better. And if you do it without bothering them, even better still.

Competes in conflict

Advancers tend to be very competitive and may see conflict as a win or lose situation. When in conflict, their first inclination is to win. They will be direct and forceful with their position. They don't like to appear weak or defeated. Even if they are wrong, they do not like to feel they are losing control or status, so they will often stand their ground. When in conflict with an Advancer, be prepared with your facts and ideas. Focus on resolving the issue as opposed to "winning" the argument. It's a subtle but important difference.

The benefits of working for an Advancer are numerous, especially if you want to work hard and advance in your career field. They are exciting, energizing people, so work is never boring or dull. They will give you challenging projects to work on that lead to real, tangible outcomes. They do not enjoy wasting time – yours or theirs – on dead-end projects or long-winded meetings. They also tend to be in the spotlight of their industry and can expose you to projects and people that could position you for advancement and opportunity.

Nonetheless, working for an Advancer certainly has drawbacks. You will be expected to work hard and possibly for long hours. You will work on their projects, not yours. You will get to see a high-achiever in action, but you will get little one-on-one time or mentorship. Also, if you disagree with your boss, you may have a challenging time reaching agreements or feeling validated in your ideas.

Proven Strategies to Manage Up the Advancer Boss

1. **Speed up!**
   Your Advancer Boss is already five steps ahead of you before you even open your mouth. You must move and speak quickly to keep pace and get their attention. Prioritize what you want to say, and get to the point. If you have less than favorable news, don't sugarcoat it. Advancers are pretty objective people and can take whatever comes their way. Give it to them straight and move on. When meeting with Advancers remember the Three Bs: Be brief, be business-like, be gone.

2. **Avoid analysis paralysis.**
   Advancers tend to be quick and pragmatic decision makers. They can easily become frustrated or annoyed by lengthy discussions or teeth gnashing over decisions. For the Advancer, perfect is often the enemy of the good. Advancers are often willing to overlook minor imperfections in favor of speed, action, and impact. Problems are only problems if they impede progress.

3. **Bring solutions, not problems.**
   The Advancer is only interested in problems that hinder results and accomplishments. And even then, they are only interested in problems if there are solutions. Therefore, when you identify a problem to your Advancer Boss you must be able to clearly articulate three things: why it is a problem, how it is affecting progress, and your idea for a solution. In fact, you should bring your Advancer Boss multiple solutions so she can decide the best path forward. For example, don't say to your Advancer, "The shared cloud system is messy and disorganized. I have trouble finding the latest documents." Instead, say, "The shared cloud is disorganized and the team has trouble finding the latest documents, which is having an impact on our ability to deliver quality work in a timely manner. If we could organize it better, we could produce higher-quality products, much faster. Here are three ideas I have come up with that can solve this problem and help us be more efficient... Let me know which one you prefer and I'll make it happen." Bam. Congratulations. You've just made your Advancer Boss fall in love with you.

4. **Request, don't complain.**
Similar to solutions over problems, Advancers hate to hear complaints. However, Advancers are open to requests. Inside every complaint is a request. Find it and make it.

5. **Don't take it personally.**
Because Advancers are driven by results and action and are focused on task accomplishment, they may not appear warm and fuzzy. In fact, they may come across as cold and uncaring. Their efforts at workplace relationship building are minimal. For Advancers, workplace relationships are built through trust and respect, and trust and respect are built by getting stuff done. It's not you, it's them.

6. **Ask what, not how.**
Remember, Advancers do not like to get bogged down in the details and planning phases of projects. If your boss is an Advancer, ask what she needs and then deliver it. Use other resources to fill in gaps on how to complete a project or just take a shot at what you think needs to be done. Your boss is most interested in the end result, so as long as you get there, an Advancer tends to be satisfied. Try brainstorming strategies with other coworkers or look to a previously successful project for a template of how your boss might want something done. Remember, above all else, Advancers respect competency, self-sufficiency, and results.

7. **Do your own homework.**
Advancers like to use their time wisely and really don't like walking through your thought process with you. If you are given a task or assignment, just take it and process the details on your own. Then do some research to fill in gaps and make a list of questions that still need to be answered. When you have an opportunity to follow up with your boss on the project, ask her only about the things that you really can't find anywhere else or that need her decision to move forward. Do as much work as you can behind the scenes and show your boss that you value her time and position.

Real-Life Story

Two years ago, I hired my first executive assistant. She's great, but almost a 180 from me in terms of personality: I'm a classic Advancer while she's more of an Evaluator. When she first started, I would give her projects and tasks, but she would always come back with a laundry list of questions. I know she wanted to please me, but I was a bit annoyed. I gave her some instructions, but mostly just asked her to figure it out on her own and then I would just change the finished product, as needed. Without me saying much, her work got better and better. When I asked her about it, she said that she would look over documents that I edited and make notes about what I had changed and do it differently the next time. She also learned to reach out to coworkers for brainstorming and guidance. Most importantly, she learned to just go with it, to create her own plan and get it done. She figured things out on her own and made stuff happen! Best. Assistant. Ever.

8. **Don't get mushy.**

    Unlike Harmonizers and Evaluators, Advancers can handle emotional responses just fine, they just don't *value* them. Getting too personal, too sensitive, or acting on feelings will erode trust and respect with your Advancer Boss. To them, too much mushiness looks like weakness. Be friendly, but don't expect to be friends. Allow plenty of time for a relationship to build. Project confidence and gain credibility with your boss before showing much of your emotional side or sharing a lot about your personal life. And please, at all costs, avoid stating your opinions with phrases like "I feel." Advancers don't care about feelings; they care about results.

9. **Don't compete for authority.**

    The last thing an Advancer Boss wants is another Advancer competing for authority and influence. Your boss likes being the boss and doesn't want to share his power or authority. Be a good follower, even if you hate it. In all likelihood, this is a great opportunity to learn from a powerful person and will set you up for your own leadership position in the future. But, for now, step back from the spotlight, let your boss make decisions, and support his ideas. Get behind his initiatives and you will find that your Advancer Boss will pull you along on a very successful path.

10. **Oppose with caution.**

Advancers respect confidence in others, but will butt heads with those who are constantly challenging their ideas or vision. Matching wits with an Advancer is asking for trouble. However, they do appreciate input from others if the approach is nonthreatening and supports the outcomes they are trying to achieve. When you need to present a differing opinion be direct, factual, and composed. Avoid becoming overly aggressive or insistent, as this may just escalate the disagreement. Don't oppose your Advancer Boss in public. Present opposing views in private whenever possible. Be ready to support your position and always present your case in service of *accomplishing their goals*.

11. **Get it done.**

At the end of the day, the Advancer Boss wants projects complete, problems solved, and questions answered. Take it upon yourself to complete your boss's priorities first and follow up with status updates. Anticipate her needs and requests – proactivity will be your best friend. Be prepared in meetings and always be ready to show your progress. Also, don't put things on the back burner hoping your boss might forget. Advancers don't usually ask for things that are not important to them. So, get started and get it done.

Working for an Advancer is hard work, which can pay off if you are up to the challenge.

The Conclusion of Veronica's Story

"Working for Heather really forced me to look for ways to be better and do better. I definitely pushed myself in ways that put me way out of my comfort zone, and she saw and appreciated it. It was hard work, I'm not going to lie. There were days when I came home from work in tears. But my efforts have definitely paid off in myriad ways: I've grown exponentially – personally and professionally, and I've enjoyed an increase in my stature within the organization and industry and my relationship with Heather.

"Sometimes it was just the little things that had the biggest impact. When we would have a meeting, I would show up with a list of things to discuss at the meeting, things that I knew were aligned with her priorities. At the same time, my peers were like, 'No, I don't really have anything to add.' They just expected Heather to bring all the topics. I also got in the habit of always being prepared and organized, thinking ahead of time what her questions were going to be or anticipating next steps. I was always the person who took things seriously, even small things. I took initiative, figured things out, and learned to do things quickly. I knew she doesn't like to waste time so I tried to be the person who could move things along and be efficient.

"I think what's changed the most is now she sees me a something of a partner. While she's definitely still the boss, there's no doubt around that, she now engages me more like a peer. She now seeks my input and asks my opinion around decisions and organizational strategies. And because over time our relationship had changed, I can be honest with her when everybody else in the room just 'Yes ma'ams' her. Now I can say things to her and give her feedback that previously I wouldn't have dreamt of. I can now be more honest with her, even if there are times when I am shaking in my boots doing it.

"What amazes me the most is that she's turned into the most influential boss I've ever had, and I've had some amazing bosses. I don't know if I would say my best boss because it's not like I enjoy it as much, but she is the boss, more than any other boss, that has moved me forward in my professional and personal growth. She's given me opportunities that I would never have had if I worked for somebody else. So even though for so long she drove me crazy, I'm probably more grateful to her than I am to anyone else I've

(continued)

(continued)

worked for because she has pushed me and helped me grow into being the leader I never thought I could be. All the things that I reacted against so negatively at first are now all the things for which I am deeply grateful."

Strategy Recap

- Speed up!
- Display competency to build respect.
- Focus on facts, tasks, and ideas rather than people.
- Be quick, focused, and to the point.
- Be prepared.
- Take initiative. Ask *what* needs to be done, not how.
- Bring solutions, not problems.
- Do what you said you would do.
- Get results and make stuff happen.

8

The Harmonizer

"The most important single ingredient in the formula of success is knowing how to get along with people."

—Theodore Roosevelt

Real-Life Story

Allison thought she had hit the jackpot when she landed her first job out of college. She was working with a small team, had flexible hours, and what seemed like the best boss ever. Allison's boss, Bill, was kind and friendly, and didn't micromanage. He mostly stayed in his office, but kept his door open and was available to talk whenever his staff had a question. Even when Allison showed up late after only two weeks on the job, Bill seemed more concerned about her well-being than about her tardiness.

However, after a few months, Allison started to become frustrated with Bill. She had noticed some inefficiencies in her team's work flow and brought them up to Bill with a number of solutions. She expected to be praised for her analysis and problem-solving skills. Instead, Bill responded with gratitude but said that he was satisfied with the team's work and that

(continued)

(continued)

some of her ideas may be outside the technical guidelines. A few more weeks went by and Allison started butting heads with the team leader, Margaret. Margaret seemed under-qualified for her position and didn't motivate the team. Allison decided to meet with Bill about her conflict with Margaret and suggested rotating the team's lead position to allow different people to gain leadership experience. Bill was nice but quickly came to Margaret's defense and said that he didn't want to disrupt the team dynamic by changing roles.

Allison felt that her ideas were good and that in other jobs she might be rewarded for her hard work and dedication to productivity. She liked many things about her work environment and her boss, but was frustrated by Bill's lack of assertiveness and feared that she would never have opportunities to grow or advance in this job.

Allison works for a Harmonizer. Harmonizers are nice people. Having a nice boss seems like a dream, but can certainly present its own challenges. A friendly boss who is focused on team cohesion can be really good for fostering workplace relationships and creating a collaborative, collegial work environment. When you have a good group of coworkers and enjoy your work, a Harmonizer Boss tends to work out pretty well. However, when there is conflict in the workplace or need for change, or you are a highly motivated, high-achieving person this type of boss may feel stifling. There is potential for all types of people to thrive with a Harmonizer Boss, but you have to understand them first.

Discover the Drivers: Understanding the Harmonizer Boss

Harmonizers like to relate

The Harmonizer Boss is people focused and functions at a slow to moderate pace. This type of person is usually calm, soft-spoken, warm, and friendly. Harmonizers tend to appear emotionally stable without showing extremes in mood, good or bad. They resist change and feel most comfortable with keeping everything steady and consistent. In the workplace, they care most about people and relationships. Most Harmonizer Bosses would prefer to have a cohesive, happy team of employees than to strive for increasing sales, innovating a new product, or beating out a competitor. Harmonizer Bosses likely get promoted into management due to their people skills, loyalty to the company, and technical expertise.

Empathetic, friendly, and accommodating

Harmonizer Bosses are known for being accommodating, cautious, and dependable. They are mostly concerned with the well-being of others and like to know those with whom they work very well. They are sensitive to the needs and feelings of others and will make changes to keep everyone happy. Harmonizers will go out of their way to create a friendly work environment but may be resistant to other changes at work. They tend to be "by the book" about following rules and regulations. They care more about safety and the feelings of others than about increasing productivity or efficiency.

Teamwork matters – a lot!

Harmonizers are motivated by high team cohesion and collaboration. Harmonizers like to feel they are contributing and helping others. They take pride in team achievements and shy away from individual recognition. They care about improvements that lead to a better, safer work environment. They work best in calm, quiet spaces where most people get along and work well together. They are happy to join team projects and enjoy meeting with others.

Averse to conflict, cautious with change

Stressors for a Harmonizer include high-risk situations, emotional extremes, and competition. Harmonizers usually avoid conflict and negative situations. For many Harmonizer Bosses, giving feedback or potentially bad news is very difficult. They may give glowing feedback to everyone just to avoid hurting someone's feelings. They also become anxious in high-pressure situations or with short deadlines.

Real-Life Story

Karen worked in health care, providing patient education with two other colleagues, Susan and Peter. Karen, Susan, and Peter all worked well together. They ate lunch together and met for after-work drinks on a regular basis. Karen considered Susan and Peter her friends. After working together for six months, Karen's supervisor was promoted and Karen was asked to fill the supervisor's role until a new person was hired for the position. Karen liked her job and, while not particularly interested in moving up, she was excited about the temporary promotion and thought it would be easy to manage Susan and Peter; after all, they were her friends. Susan and Peter were both interested in applying for the supervisor position and were jealous that Karen was picked after such a short time in the job. Susan and Peter were very competitive, and each spent time in Karen's office every day telling her why he or she would be better for the position than the other. The relationship between the three colleagues eroded quickly, and Karen became very anxious at work.

One day, Susan and Peter got into a heated argument in the patient waiting room. Karen tried to diffuse the situation by talking in a calm voice and telling both Susan and Peter that they were great candidates and equally qualified for the position. Although still angry, Peter took a short break to calm down and then asked Karen for a meeting at the end of the day. In the meantime, Susan followed Karen back to her office and spent an hour venting her frustration and listing all the reasons that Peter was a poor choice for the supervisor position. In her afternoon meeting with Peter, he apologized for his behavior and explained how he wished they could both be promoted and shared his ideas for ongoing collaboration. Karen thought that both Susan and Peter were qualified for the position, but in the end, she recommended Peter for his ability to control his emotions and for putting the team before himself.

(continued on page 71)

Proven Strategies to Manage Up the Harmonizer Boss

1. **Focus on the team.**
   Your boss is happiest when the team is working well together and everyone is getting along. Do your part to establish and maintain harmony. If you have a conflict with someone, try to work directly with that person to resolve it. If you constantly go to your boss for interpersonal conflict issues, he will probably disappoint you with his response and you will likely lose favor over time. Aim suggestions at improving team cohesion and morale, not singling someone out. Even if you don't care much about how others feel, fake it! Your boss will appreciate your concern for others and the team will benefit from it.

2. **Don't be a drama queen.**
   Harmonizers don't do very well with inconsistent emotions or behaviors. Remember, your Harmonizer Boss performs best in a calm, peaceful environment. Anger, sadness, or even too much exuberance may stress her out. If you need to have an emotional response to a situation, confide in a friend or loved one before storming into your boss's office. Regain your composure and speak calmly to your boss to get her attention on what you are trying to say, instead of your reaction.

3. **Think about safety.**
   Do you have a laundry list of ideas that go nowhere with your Harmonizer Boss? Try reframing them in terms of how a change could enhance safety or stability for you, your team, or your customers. It also helps to know the rules and regulations that apply to your workplace or industry. Your boss is focused on adhering to guidelines and keeping everyone safe (and happy). If you can explain how your suggestion is within standards and helps with safety, you will have your boss's ear.

4. **Help them make decisions.**
   Your Harmonizer Boss may delay decision making until she feels like she has a perfect answer – which may be too late. Do your part by offering to research a topic or read through company policies. If it is a big decision for your department, discuss forming a committee. Your boss loves to work on teams, and having support and buy-in from others will help her reach a conclusion faster.

5. **Be a people person.**

   Even if you are perfectly happy working alone in your office, make a point to develop personal relationships with others in your workplace. Eat lunch in the break room, attend social events, and show sincere interest in your coworkers and your boss. This might be completely against your nature, but it is worth it. Your boss will notice that you share his concern for others and will value your efforts.

6. **Slow down.**

   Harmonizer Bosses are often methodical people. If you barrage them with all your ideas at once or jump from one suggestion to the next, they will feel overwhelmed and shut down. Introduce one idea at a time and provide plenty of detail, steps to accomplish the task, and how you will collaborate with others. Then, give them time to mull it over before following up. You may have to be patient, but over time your ideas will be heard and you may be given more latitude to change things on your own in the future.

7. **Challenge and reward yourself.**

   Your boss is not likely to single you out for a great opportunity or reward you for your hard work. A Harmonizer Boss will not be ungrateful, but is more prone to applaud the success of the team and assign group projects. You will need to motivate yourself if you have lofty aspirations for career success. Look for an exciting training course, set a goal for your team, or look for a new client to pursue. Structure your ideas around the team, and your boss will probably bite. Then, when you reach a goal, finish a course, secure a new client, reward yourself! Make sure to keep track of your contributions to add to your résumé and to help your boss write a stellar letter of recommendation, should you ever need one.

8. **Find a mentor.**

   Look around for a mentor who is in the next stage of your career and has a different workstyle from your boss. This may be someone in a different department or a different company altogether. It will help you rely less on your boss for professional development and can help you gain leadership skills that your boss may lack. Remember, you care more about your career than anyone else, and you cannot depend on your boss to provide everything you need to advance.

Real-Life Story *(continued from page 68)*

Allison thought about looking for a new job, but really didn't want to leave her first "real" job after less than a year. She reached out to a former professor and mentor, Sarah, to ask for advice. After meeting with Sarah, Allison had a few strategies to try. First, she wrote down each of her ideas and drafted detailed steps for implementing a change, listed how the change would benefit her team, and described how the outcomes would improve safety and team cohesion. Then, she presented the ideas one at a time (with several months between each) to her boss, Bill, asked him to think about it, and scheduled a follow-up meeting a week later.

Bill showed interest in her first idea, but hesitated a bit about making a change. Allison suggested introducing the idea to the team to discuss. Bill loved the idea, and soon they were having monthly team meetings to specifically discuss new ideas. Allison also made an effort to work through her conflict with Margaret. They chatted over coffee and Allison soon learned that Margaret was unhappy with her job and was looking for a position in another department. Margaret found a new job several months later and Allison was promoted to the team's lead position.

Strategy Recap

- Be a team player and show genuine concern for your boss and coworkers.
- Approach change and conflict slowly and with a cool head.
- Offer support for decision making and include others.
- Avoid venting in front of your boss; find other outlets to express your emotions.
- Show how your ideas improve safety or team cohesion.
- Keep track of your own successes and look for ways to build your résumé.

9

The Evaluator

"If a task has once begun. Never leave it till it's done. Be the labor great or small. Do it well or not at all."

—Anonymous

Real-Life Story

Chrystal works for a professional services firm and her new boss, Brenda, is driving her crazy. Brenda is nice enough and seems to really care about her job and the work produced by her team. But Chrystal often feels that Brenda is constantly looking over her shoulder and doesn't let her do her job. Brenda asks a lot of questions and never seems satisfied with the updates that Chrystal provides. Chrystal thinks that Brenda is too detail oriented and is not very adaptable with different people. She has one style and treats everyone the same way.

One day, Chrystal was leading a call with a client to review the client project plan and timeline. Before the call, Chrystal met with Brenda and updated her on the meeting agenda and project timeline. During the call, though, Brenda kept interrupting to ask for more detail and in the course of the meeting, changed the project timeline and action items. Chrystal felt defeated, micromanaged, and distrusted.

Everybody likes things to be right but nobody needs it more than the Evaluator Boss. The Evaluator Boss is driven by producing high-quality, accurate work at all costs. Often slow and methodical, Evaluators value getting things right through logic and proven processes. They will often question everything to the extent that it will feel as though they are micromanaging your work. This is one of the leading qualities of Evaluator Bosses. They will ask a lot of questions to make sure everything is logical and will take all of the time necessary to complete the research to answer all of these questions. In some cases, it can be great to have a boss who is slow to make decisions and seeks to find the most accurate solution. But in many situations, this boss can be frustrating, especially for those who are creative, energetic, and fast paced.

Discovering the Drivers: Understanding the Evaluator Boss

The office is for work

The Evaluator Boss is focused on tasks, not people, and views time spent at work primarily for completing a series of tasks. Evaluators tend to work alone and can spend hours on end glued to their computer screen. They feel best when they accomplish a goal or make significant progress on a project. Evaluators do not view work as a place to make and build relationships, and they often get frustrated when their time is used for meetings or socializing. Evaluator Bosses are likely to engage with employees on an as-needed basis to answer questions or provide instructions, but they typically do not participate in small talk or spend much time nurturing or developing their staff.

Good enough is not good enough

Evaluators are often described as perfectionists and value precision and accuracy in their work (and yours). Although Evaluators like to get work completed, they tend to be slow and cautious to ensure that the work is done correctly. They hate making mistakes and don't tolerate mistakes or sloppy work in others, either. They believe that if something is worth doing, it is worth doing well, and to that end they usually do not support a lot of creative or innovative ideas that are thrown together hastily. An Evaluator Boss may come across as a micromanager or nitpicker in her efforts to perfect a document, even an e-mail! In addition, Evaluators set very high standards and tend to be overly critical of themselves and others.

Methods, logic, and analysis

Evaluators rely on logic and reason to make decisions and to understand new information. They live in a world of facts and need time to process, research, and analyze before they feel comfortable implementing something new or even taking a step in a new direction. To an Evaluator, to do anything on a whim or with a "gut feeling" is foolish. An Evaluator Boss will likely appear to lack creativity and will tend to shut down around those who like to brainstorm and are always coming up with new ideas. In fact, Evaluators are often skeptical of ideas that are not backed by details, facts, and references. The upside is that when an Evaluator implements a new process it is usually successful because he has exhaustively tested the idea for flaws. However, some good ideas may get passed over for lack of data-driven support, and others may just get missed altogether due to the slow nature of the Evaluator's response time. Working with the Evaluator Boss can be frustrating when a quick decision must be made.

Robotically objective

If you work with or for an Evaluator, you may wonder if Evaluators ever have an emotional response to anything. They will usually appear calm and cool-headed and approach situations with objectivity. In dealing with conflict, they will see it as a disagreement over who is correct; they don't really mind if it is them, they just want to identify the right answer. Although this sounds like a nice quality in a boss, it can be very frustrating to resolve a conflict without any of the "human element" or sensitivity of other personality types. Related to this, the Evaluator does not do very well in handling erratic behavior or emotional extremes. To an Evaluator, every problem has a solution and there is no point in having a personal or subjective reaction to it. Remember, they are "evaluators," not "feelers." For example, when considering how a layoff may affect the workforce or the effects of deploying 25 percent of the workforce to a new regional location, their focus is objectively what makes best logical sense and nothing more. That is partly why you need them and partly why you have a hard time with them.

Real-Life Story

Calvin and Amy have a difficult working relationship. Calvin is an Evaluator who is often frustrated by Amy's approach to work. While Calvin values a methodical, logical, calm, and solitary approach to projects, Amy is driven by passion, collaboration, and inspiration. Since Calvin is her supervisor, Amy has had to learn to tone down her exuberance and interact with Calvin in a more formal, dispassionate manner. "It's been really hard for me to work for Calvin. I've always had bosses who appreciated my enthusiasm and relationship building so it took me by surprise that what had always been an asset at work was now a drawback. It took me some time to get my head around it, but now I see that in order to be successful with Calvin, I need to adapt to his style. I can't say it is easy for me, but once I realized that my approach was negatively impacting our relationship, I now work really hard to be more measured and systematic. When I am excited or passionate about an idea, instead of bombarding Calvin, I reach out to other colleagues to brainstorm or blue sky. This allows me to present my ideas to Calvin in a way that he can hear them and appreciate them. He's definitely not my ideal boss, but I know that I can make this work."

There are many benefits to this type of boss, starting with the fact that they value accuracy and will reward this type of behavior when they see it in others. This is also how they begin to trust others they work with because they know the decisions or strategies were based in logic, fact, and objectivity. They are detail oriented and will take on the extra work to make sure things are done accurately and correctly. The Evaluator Boss will develop plans and timelines to assist everyone with getting the work done right. While this last one may tend to be a nuisance at times, it can also catch things that others on the team haven't thought of.

Drawbacks for the Evaluator Boss can be hard to see because everything they do is done in an effort to be accurate. However, their drawbacks are just as numerous as with any other boss. First, they tend to focus so much on the details of the task that they can lose sight of the big picture. Proverbially speaking, they can sometimes miss the forest for the trees. In addition, they question *everything*. These questions can get in the way of meeting deadlines or can hold projects up unnecessarily. Evaluator Bosses are not good at addressing issues that surprise them. They need the time to think about the issues and do the appropriate research to be able to deliver a thoughtful, accurate response. Last, they tend to be long-winded once you get them talking. This is because they feel the need to give you all of the information they researched to justify their logical, accurate, and objective decision.

Proven Strategies to Manage Up the Evaluator Boss

1. **Avoid surprises.**

   Evaluators do not like to be put on the spot. They like to have ample time to think about a topic and gather the facts before weighing in. If you want to discuss a new idea or project, warn them ahead of time. Even better, schedule a meeting and provide a list of topics at least a few days out. If you already have a regular meeting with your Evaluator Boss do not surprise him by asking for input on things he didn't expect to be discussing. Create an agenda or send a simple e-mail the day before with a list of items you would like to discuss.

2. **Be prepared.**

   If you are passionate about a particular aspect of your work, or you want to inject some creativity into a project, you need to do your homework before unloading all of your ideas on your boss. Without details and facts, your boss is going to be skeptical of anything new and dismiss it for lack of factual support. Brainstorm ideas alone or with a colleague and then research your top options to show your boss that you've thought them through. Your boss will want to see statistics, facts, and any evidence to back up your proposal. In addition, show her how the change will create order, accuracy, reliability, or increase quality. Provide all this in a written format first and then ask to present your idea or meet to discuss it.

3. **Raise your standards.**

   You probably already work very hard and want to produce quality work. That being said, your Evaluator Boss likely has even higher standards. They are perfectionists, after all! Try your best to focus your energy on just a few projects at a time and pay close attention to detail. If you don't have an eye for formatting, ask a colleague to review your documents or make a checklist of all of the items (font, spacing, margins, etc.) to review before submitting a report. Your Evaluator Boss thinks that anything worth doing is worth doing well, so put in the extra effort to make your work look polished and thorough.

4. **Focus on the facts.**
   Remember that your Evaluator Boss uses data, not feelings or impulses, to make decisions. Whether that decision is to approve your vacation plans, authorize funding for new equipment, or give you a raise, this boss needs information. If you can show your boss that your request makes logical, rational sense, he is more willing to agree with you. If you think you deserve a raise, do some research on salary for similar positions, document your most recent and significant contributions, and demonstrate how you plan to continue to contribute with greater responsibility. Asking for a raise for personal reasons or getting emotional will likely get you nowhere.

5. **Slow down.**
   Be patient, persistent, and diplomatic. Evaluators need time to think, so give them what they need. Some decisions may have shorter timelines than others, but try to give your boss as much time as possible. Provide timelines and schedules to help structure the decision-making process and to keep important or short turnaround items high in the queue. If your boss has questions or requests more information, act right away to find the answers. Your boss may appear to be stalling, but keep in mind that she can become very stressed by making "rash" decisions.

6. **Impress with detail.**
   While some bosses (like Advancers and Energizers) are easily bored with details, Evaluators thrive on them. Make sure you have command of the details and are prepared to demonstrate this knowledge at a moment's notice. They need more than the headline or bottom line. They need it all.

7. **Respect the process.**
   Because Evaluators value quality over everything, they are generally big proponents of process. To them, processes exist to ensure

high-quality results. Skirting proven processes is abhorrent (and dangerous) to them. They are the classic "measure twice, cut once" types. Rather than try to skirt a process established by an Evaluator, find ways to enhance the process – just make sure your suggested changes are backed up by data and are framed in a way that improves the quality of the output.

8. **Manage your emotions.**
Your boss views everything through an objective lens and has a difficult time factoring in emotions. This is especially true during conflict. If you have a disagreement with your boss, you will need to show that you are right to win him over. Give him details and facts to support your position in a calm, neutral way. Also, try to view his position from the same perspective. Your boss rarely makes a decision or implements a change without a tedious process to determine the right answer. However, his approach may seem cold or unfeeling. Your best bet is to do your part to understand your boss's outlook, provide him with support for your position, and find another outlet to vent your frustrations.

9. **Learn from criticism.**
Evaluator bosses can be highly critical of work products. They love to poke holes and identify potential and real problems and mistakes. This is not the same thing as being critical of you as a person. Learn to accept their work product critiques without taking it personally, even if it feels harsh or insensitive. Take the time to learn from their experience and expertise. Learn to anticipate their hole-poking and come prepared with solutions and answers.

Real-Life Story

Chrystal was able to (albeit begrudgingly) slowly respect, accept, and even adapt to Brenda's style. Once she shifted her attitude from annoyance to curiosity, she realized that working for Brenda has helped make her a better consultant. "Once I stopped resenting Brenda and feeling sorry for myself, I realized that Brenda had a lot to teach me and that her attention to detail was helping me raise the quality of my work. I've learned that when I present

(continued)

(continued)

ideas and solutions to Brenda for a client engagement, Brenda's first instinct is to point out all the potential pitfalls, problems, and shortcomings of my strategy. This has forced me to be much more robust in my thinking and planning. Before presenting my ideas to Brenda (or the client) I now take the time to critically review and poke holes in my own ideas. And as much as I hate to admit it, I've been thinking a lot about how to create better processes for myself to ensure consistent high-quality work."

Strategy Recap

- Do your homework and provide your boss with as much detail as possible.
- Focus on producing fewer but better projects, and pay attention to detail.
- Give your Evaluator Boss plenty of time to respond to requests.
- Avoid emotional responses and try to stay objective in conflict.
- Learn to love facts and support your ideas with evidence.
- Separate work criticism from personal criticism – it's not about you as a person!

10

Difficult Bosses

"Happy families are all alike; every unhappy family is unhappy in its own way."
—Leo Tolstoy, *Anna Karenina*

If you stay in the workforce long enough, at some point you are going to experience a difficult boss. Because most organizations still promote people based on their technical skills and not their managerial aptitude, you are more likely to experience mediocre or difficult bosses than great bosses. While this is unfortunate, it doesn't have to be the end of the world or a roadblock in your career. Learning to deal with a difficult boss is a great skill to develop. Learning to manage a difficult boss means being able to adapt a strategic perspective. Learning to manage a difficult boss requires you to work a little harder, reflect a little more, and make conscious choices.

Great bosses share lots of similar traits; they are trustworthy, encouraging, empathetic, engaged, supportive, knowledgeable, communicative, fair, respectful, and motivating, just to name a few. They make work rewarding, happy, and positive. We feel engaged and supported. The difficult boss, however, comes in many shades, flavors, and complexities. Most difficult and dysfunctional bosses are composed of multiple personality traits and behaviors, some good, some bad. Your boss may be kind, but controlling. He may be trustworthy, but not very smart. She may be loyal, but nitpicky. He might be motivational, but overbearing. She may be engaged, but not very decisive. He may be super knowledgeable, but completely uncommunicative. And the list goes on. When dealing with difficult bosses, it is important to identify, understand, and navigate those *behaviors* you find difficult.

Since humans (and bosses are humans, too) interact with the world using a continuum of behaviors, difficult boss personalities usually result from the underuse or overuse of certain behaviors. This overuse or underuse can turn perfectly fine behaviors – when used in appropriate and moderate ways – into difficult ones. For example, a boss who is able to delegate is a great thing, when used appropriately. But when that boss delegates too much she runs the risk of being too hands off, too disengaged. On the other side of the continuum is the boss who doesn't delegate enough, thus causing him to show up as controlling, micromanaging, or nitpicking.

While there are far too many shades of difficult bosses to put into one book, I have identified the top 10 difficult bosses you are likely to encounter in today's workforce. These are the boss personalities that seem to be the most common and the most annoying for most people:

- Micromanagers
- Ghosts
- Impulsives
- Narcissists
- Pushovers
- Best Friends
- Workaholics
- Incompetents
- Seagulls and Nitpickers
- The Truly Terrible: Psychos, Tyrants, and Bullies

Because people are never 100 percent of anything 100 percent of the time, you may find that your "mostly great" boss has one or several of these tendencies in moderation. Or conversely, you may find that your boss has several to many of these tendencies or that they are so far off the spectrum in one (or more) tendencies that they have gone from being difficult to being impossible to work for. They may have become the "boss from hell." As you read through the strategies in the following chapters on how to manage up these difficult boss types, please keep in mind the following overarching perspectives about dealing with difficult bosses.

Appreciate the opportunity, embrace the challenge

Yes, you heard me. Embrace and appreciate. Why? Because you will learn and grow more from a difficult boss than you ever will from a great or easy boss. A difficult boss will challenge you in more ways than you can imagine. If you take up that challenge, you will learn a great deal about your own resiliency, values, likes, dislikes, strengths, weaknesses, and flexibility. You will learn strategies to navigate other difficult people in your life, including coworkers, neighbors, friends, relatives, and yes, even significant others. But the most important thing you will learn is what kind of leader *you want to be when it is your turn.* Nearly everyone interviewed for this book said their best leadership teacher was their worst boss. The experience may be terrible, but the lessons can be priceless.

Identify the difficult behavior

Rather than label your boss a difficult person, try to identify the difficult behavior or behaviors. This will help you break down the problem into smaller, more manageable bits. Once we label a whole person as difficult, we lose our ability to make strategic choices about the actual behavior that is a problem. If your boss is a micromanager then develop strategies that address that particular dysfunction. Remember, we can't change other people; we can only try to meet them where they are and change the way we interact with them.

Assume positive intent (the best you can)

This one may be hard, but is extremely helpful as it will open you up to more strategic choices. Not every difficult boss is an evil person. In fact, more often than not, many difficult boss behaviors result from a lack of self-awareness, a lack of emotional intelligence, or a lack of basic managerial know-how, rather than from an evil intent. Unless your boss is truly a psychopath, then chances are he thinks he is doing the right thing. And, why wouldn't he? The organization rewards bosses' behavior by keeping them in their jobs.

Own your rub

While some behaviors are universally difficult – such as screaming, bullying, lying, and cheating – other behaviors may be more difficult for some of us than others. For example, if you are a highly independent, self-starting, experienced worker, then you may be much more sensitive to being managed than someone with much less experience or confidence. What feels like too much to you may be just right for someone else. Understanding yourself is always the first step to successfully dealing with difficult people.

Seek to understand

All human behavior stems from some inner drive, want, or need. The more you can figure out what the inner driver is, the better you can align your strategy to meet that need. While it may feel self-satisfying (and fun!) to judge that need, judging isn't going to help you flex. When we come from a place of judgment, we become stuck in our own worldview. When we come from a place of curiosity we expand our range of possibility. As the French author Marcel Proust famously said, "The only real voyage of discovery consists not in seeking new landscapes, but in having new eyes." Put on new eyes and see what you can discover. It may surprise you.

Decide what you can live with

One of the most important questions you must ask yourself is, "Can I live with this behavior?" In other words, is this difficult behavior a deal breaker for you or can you somehow make it work? Do you want to make it work? Would you want to work for a petulant, egotistical, uncompromising micromanager who frequently rants, threatens, and makes embarrassing outbursts against his employees? Probably not. Unless that person was Steve Jobs. Although Jobs's management style was notorious for these qualities and difficult, to say the least, tens of thousands of people decided that they could live with it. Only you can decide if dealing with difficult behavior is worth it. Stay in a place of choice, because a place of choice is an empowered place.

11

The Micromanager

"The wise adapt themselves to circumstances, as water molds itself to the pitcher."
—Chinese proverb

Real-Life Story

Mia was at her wit's end. As the program director for a medium-sized non-profit, she was responsible for creating and executing programs and reported directly to the founder and executive director. Although Mia was an experienced program director with many years of experience, her boss needed to see and approve everything that Mia produced. Every memo, every project, and every programmatic decision had to be reviewed and approved. Although her title was "Director" Mia wasn't allowed to direct anything. She had no autonomy and no opportunity to use her experience or expertise. Instead she simply took orders and functioned as an assistant. She hated it.

Nobody likes to be micromanaged. Having someone draped over your shoulder, constantly scrutinizing your every move is frustrating and soul crushing. Human beings have an innate neuropsychological need for some level of autonomy, so a boss who denies you this can be very difficult on both an emotional level and a workplace engagement level. In addition to being incredibly frustrating, having an overcontrolling boss can and will stunt your professional growth and development. Micromanagers who dictate and control your every move prevent you from exercising independent thought, creative problem solving, and risk taking – all things that lead to growth.

Being micromanaged is always the number one pet peeve that people talk about in our workshops. It seems that everyone has a horror story about having worked for a micromanager. Here are actual complaints about micromanaging bosses that we've heard from participants in our workshops:

- He always needs to know where I am and what I am working on.
- She tells me in great detail how to complete every assignment, even ones in which I am the expert.
- He constantly scrutinizes my work and checks in constantly on my progress.
- Nothing is ever good enough unless it's done exactly her way.
- He is totally swamped but he won't delegate anything.
- She'll give me an assignment, and then after I've worked on it, she takes it away and does it herself.
- He's a total control freak.
- I'm not allowed to work on anything without her permission.
- He only gives me enough information I need for each discrete part of the assignment. This means I have to constantly check in with him for additional information to complete the project.
- My supervisor never trusts my judgment. I constantly have to justify the few decisions I am allowed to make.
- I'm so afraid of making a mistake that I now just sit and wait until she asks for something.
- Everybody complains about our boss's micromanagement. We've started a self-help drinking group.

Sound familiar? Micromanaging is one of the most prevalent management dysfunctions in the workplace. The good news is that it is also one of the easiest to deal with. The first step is to try to understand the source of the behavior. The second step is to employ strategies to work with a micromanager.

Discover the Drivers: Understanding the Micromanager

Micromanaging is often the result of a combination of internal and external drivers, both emotional and situational.

Insecurity/Neuroticism

Many bosses micromanage from a state of emotional insecurity. Some people elevated to management become insecure about their ability to succeed. Others are just innately neurotic or high strung. People who are insecure about their own abilities often attempt to counteract those feelings by becoming overcontrolling. This illusion of power helps them ease their own sense of inadequacy. In addition, some people tend to be OCD in their attention to details. This does not make them bad people, just people with specific needs. At the end of the day, these behaviors are all about fear. Meeting the needs of people who are insecure or neurotic means assuaging their fears through your behaviors, words, and actions. Trust is key.

Perfectionism/Extremely High Standards

Some managers – either by nature or nurture – will show up as perfectionists or control freaks. Sometimes it is their natural proclivity; these are the people who seek perfection and control in everything they do, personally or professionally. Their motto is, "If it's worth doing, it's worth doing right." Other times this perfectionism and control are driven by the reality of their organizational role, the powers that be above them, the corporate culture, and the nature of the work itself. There are many fields where exactitude is necessary and mistakes are verboten or just plain dangerous. If you, as a manager, are told that your clients' success depends on you getting everything right, you might become a controlling perfectionist, too. The corporate culture might encourage micromanagement. Whatever the driver may be for the perfectionist, managing up to a Micromanager who expects perfection means adapting to and adopting those high standards yourself. It means consistently delivering mistake-free, high-quality work. Every time.

Seek to Understand the Behavior

In order to get a sense of what might be driving your boss, put on your boss detective hat and ask yourself some questions:

o Have you built trust with your boss? Do you know how to do that? Do you know what drives your boss's criteria for trust?

o Is your boss a perfectionist?

o Do you operate in an environment or culture where mistakes are unacceptable or even dangerous?

o Is your boss under pressure from above? What kind of pressure?

o Does your boss work for someone who is a Micromanager or a perfectionist?

o Does your boss have enough of her own work to do? Or does she have too much time on her hands?

o Does your boss micromanage all projects or just certain ones? If only in certain situations, when does he tend to slip into micromanagement?

o Do I have micromanagement tendencies myself? If so, when does this occur or what would drive this behavior in me? What would I need from others to let go of this behavior?

o Is your boss a new hire or newly promoted?

o Does your boss micromanage all employees or just you?

Once you have a sense of what might be driving the micromanaging behavior (and it might be multiple things) you can start implementing strategies to build trust, mitigate fear, and proactively deliver the level of quality and perfection your boss desires.

Proven Strategies to Manage Up the Micromanager

1. **Do not resist.**
    Instead, dig in and manage up. Stop being surprised by this behavior. The truth about overcoming this managerial dysfunction is that it requires you to do more in the short run in order to gain more in the long run. It will initially add work to your plate and will require you to put in a bit more effort. Micromanaging doesn't go away overnight. Your boss isn't going to wake up one day and announce, "I think I will stop crushing the souls of my staff." No. Micromanaging can only be alleviated by your choices and

behaviors, and it only lessens once your boss has confidence and trust in your ability to meet his or her needs. It will only go away when your boss's fears are assuaged.

2. **Stay one step ahead.**
   The two keys words to successfully manage up to a Micromanager are "anticipation" and "proaction." The more you can anticipate your boss's wants, needs, and expectations and proactively address them, the sooner you can remove the opportunity or need for them to micromanage. If you know that every quarter a certain project or report is due, then several weeks before the project is due start letting your boss know that it is on your radar and to-do list. Anticipate what Micromanagers want and be proactive in giving it to them.

3. **Develop trust.**
   Much of micromanaging is based on fear, so you must develop trust with your boss. Instilling trust means to impart a sense of confidence that you can and will deliver what the boss wants and needs. Your boss must trust your judgment, your ability to meet her goals and expectations, and your ability to consistently deliver quality work. Gaining the trust of a Micromanager means being a consistent performer, so be sure you are delivering on your end.

4. **Keep your boss (overly) informed:**
   Provide regular updates, and status and progress reports *before* your boss asks for them. This could look like a daily e-mail or memo that lists all your projects and their status. If your boss is concerned about your time or efficiency, then make sure your boss knows how you are spending your time. If you are going to be late, let him know. If you have a client coffee, let him know. If you are staying late to work on a project, let him know. Keeping your boss fully informed and in the loop builds trust and security.

5. **Important stuff first.**
   Make sure you know what is most important to your boss and address those items first. If you are providing regular updates, make sure you put what is important to your boss up front in your communication.

6. **Seek feedback and don't take it personally.**
   When you deliver projects, or are being overly instructed on how to do something, resist the urge to get angry. Instead, get curious.

Ask your boss about their preferences. Find out *why* they prefer that approach. Ask what you can do to make it even better. Find out what "right the first time" actually means. To do this, you must remove any trace of antagonism or resentment from your words, your body language, and your vocal tone. To pull this off, you must put yourself in a true place of curiosity and learning.

7. **Deliver high-quality work every time.**

   Double- and triple-check everything you do before giving it to your boss. Learn what markers of quality your boss wants/needs and her preferences. If your boss hates the Oxford comma, then drop it. If your boss prefers a certain font, then use it. If your boss expects projects delivered 24 hours ahead of the due date, then do it. If your boss wants covers on all the TPS reports, then provide them. As ridiculous as *you* may think it is, the more you deliver exactly what your boss wants in the way she wants it, the sooner she will stop looking over your shoulder to tell you.

8. **Ask and recap.**

   When your boss gives you an assignment, ask lots of questions up front. Try to get as much information as you can. Develop a list of questions that you can always ask. You want to discover as best you can:

   o The context of the assignment (what and why this is needed),
   o The parameters of the assignment (what it needs to include/not include),
   o The deadline (when it is due to *her*),
   o How much review she needs and when,
   o Who else may need to contribute to the project, and
   o Her preferences for approach and execution.

   In short, what does successful completion of this project look like to her? Once you have this information, take a few minutes to recap to make sure you heard the information correctly. I'm a big fan of a written (via e-mail or memo) recap. Not only does this help your boss feel heard but it also provides an opportunity for your boss to reflect on the information she provided, and it may trigger additional information sharing.

9. **Learn and attend to their concerns.**

   Pay attention to what really matters to your boss. Pay attention to their fears and idiosyncrasies. Learn what matters to your boss's boss and what they are being held accountable for. If your boss hates it when he can't find you, take a moment to let your boss know when you are stepping away from your desk. A quick text or e-mail does the trick: "Hey, boss, I'm running out for a coffee. Be back in 10 minutes. Can I get you one?" If your boss is concerned about mistakes, then make sure you let her know the procedures that you have in place to mitigate mistakes. Better yet, try to come up with additional processes and strategies that can help everyone avoid mistakes.

10. **Look inside.**

    Are you the only one complaining about your boss's micromanaging? If so, then take a good, hard, honest look at your performance. Take an objective look at your attitude, productivity, efficiency, work quality, and track record. Do you slide in projects moments before the deadline? Does your work consistently need multiple revisions? Do you only provide updates to your boss when he asks? Have you done everything you can to proactively instill confidence in your boss about your work? What are you doing that is keeping your boss (not any boss – *this particular boss*) from trusting you?

    Not sure how to self-evaluate? Try these tips: For the next two weeks, take a few minutes after completing each task or project to review your work from your boss's perspective. Avoid the trap of saying to yourself, "Well, if **I** were the boss, here is what **I'd** look for." Instead, say to yourself, "If I were **my** boss, what would he or she look for?" It's a subtle but important difference. You must review your work from the eyes of **your** boss, not from your eyes as if **you** were the boss. Reflect on your general workplace disposition. Are there areas where you can improve? Be more efficient? Communicate more effectively? Ask more questions? Be more proactive? Improve timeliness? Be rigorous and honest in your self-evaluation, and then take action.

11. **Look around.**

    Are there coworkers who your boss leaves alone? Are some people allowed autonomy? If so, reflect on what they do differently. Learn and adopt their strategies.

Real-Life Story

Joyce was a supervisor in a manufacturing plant. She noticed that while the plant manager micromanaged her and her team, there were other teams and supervisors who were given much more latitude and autonomy. So, Joyce investigated. She quickly learned that the other supervisors created daily "stretch goals" for their teams and reported these goals and their results to the boss on a daily basis. While these goals were informal, it provided the plant manager with the sense that those teams were engaged and proactively addressing productivity enhancements. Joyce quickly adopted the same strategy. After a couple of weeks, Joyce, too, was enjoying more autonomy and trust. It was a simple matter of discovering what the boss wanted and then delivering it.

12. **Give it time.**

Finally, building trust is a matter of time. If you are new to your job, then the micromanaging may alleviate itself once the boss feels you have a thorough understanding of the job, the work, and the organization. Staying proactive and being willing to be a learner will help you move through this stage. Take the time to really learn what your boss needs and give it to her. Newly hired or newly promoted managers are often insecure in their new roles, which often leads to micromanaging, at least in the short term. Show your boss through words and deeds that you are there to help her and the department succeed. Offer suggestions diplomatically and tactfully. Often, familiarity and confidence with her role and the team is all that is needed to mitigate the micromanagement. Give your Micromanager time to get used to you and trust you before you start pushing for change or autonomy.

Real-Life Story

After a few soul-crushing months of being micromanaged, Mia started providing daily memos to her boss that listed all the projects she was working on, the status of those projects, and any problems or challenges she was facing.

At first, the boss would send Mia's memo back to her with "See me!" written in red (of course). Mia feared her strategy had backfired. Instead of gaining more autonomy, Mia feared that she had actually lost ground. After a few "see me" meetings, it suddenly dawned on Mia that the order of the projects listed in her memo mattered. Mia quickly revamped her daily project memo and started listing the projects and tasks that she knew her boss cared about the most (regardless of their actual level of importance or priority) first. The impact was immediate. Mia stopped getting "See me" messages. In fact, over time, Mia was able to decrease the frequency of her project communiqués. Over a few months, Mia went from daily memos to every other day, then twice a week, and finally to one simple weekly update.

Mia is convinced that it was these consistent updates and attention to her boss's priorities that gained her the freedom and autonomy that she wanted and needed. Mia couldn't believe it was so simple. Yes, it took a little extra time on her part, but she discovered that not only did it help alleviate her boss's micromanagement but the memos began to serve as her master to-do list, helping her focus even more on the things that needed to get done. In addition, two more unintended but positive consequences occurred: Mia learned that she was also able to "sneak in" cool projects that in the past her boss would have shut down (listed at the end, of course). The other benefit was when Mia decided it was time to leave, these memos provided a great record of her projects, which made updating her résumé and preparing for interviews easy and painless.

Strategy Recap

- Anticipate and act.
- Learn about and attend to your boss's concerns.
- Work to build trust and rapport.
- Keep your Micromanager informed and in the loop.
- Stay one step ahead.
- Overwhelm your boss with the data he wants.
- Make sure you put what is important to your boss up front.
- Update frequently.
- Ask for specifics up front.
- Look at your own behavior.
- Look at your coworkers.
- Be consistent and patient.

12

The Hands-Off, Absentee, Ghost Boss

"Be content with what you have; rejoice in the way things are. When you realize there is nothing lacking, the whole world belongs to you."

—Lao Tzu, *Tao Te Ching*

Confession Time

I tend to be a bit of a Ghost Boss myself. As an introverted workaholic, I often get completely consumed with my own projects and will frequently go days without having any substantial conversations with my team. For the most part, my team enjoys the independence that this affords them on individual projects. However, there are also times when my ghosting causes confusion and bottlenecks. My staff has done a great job of taking ownership of managing this dynamic. They have taken it upon themselves to request, schedule, and pin me down with regular team meetings. They know how to get my attention if a matter is urgent – they text me. They know how to keep me in the loop on stuff that is not urgent – they e-mail me. And when

(continued)

(continued)

they need something that requires a quick conversation – they call me. When they need a lengthier conversation, they put themselves on my calendar. They know that I am more receptive to longer conversations in the late afternoon after I've had time to make a dent in my own to-do list. I suspect they have even figured out that if they want to pitch me a new idea or ask a favor, they should call me after 6 p.m. when, chances are, I'm sipping my evening glass of sauvignon blanc. The point is, my team learned my style, and they manage up accordingly.

While being micromanaged is difficult, being *under*managed presents its own host of problems. On the one hand, a hands-off, absentee, macro-managing boss can be exciting, energizing, and empowering, especially for independent types who thrive on the freedom to execute their tasks with little interference. On the other hand, it can be frustrating, scary, and nerve-racking for those who may need or want more guidance and support. Love them or hate them, the hands-off or Ghost Boss can be a dream or a nightmare, depending on the level of support and guidance that *you* need to be successful.

Discover the Drivers: Understanding the Ghost Boss

There are several types of hands-off bosses and many reasons why they ghost. Some revel in giving their employees autonomy, freedom, and flexibility while others are just plain checked out, apathetic, lazy, uninterested, or retired in place. Before determining what strategies to use to manage up your Ghost Boss, take a moment to identify the type of ghost you have on your hands. The types are very different:

The hands-off/macro-manager boss

This supervisor style is the complete opposite of the Micromanager. The hands-off boss takes pride in being a macro-manager by delegating and empowering. They consciously remain hands off in order to provide their staff with freedom, flexibility, and autonomy. They want you to be an independent self-starter. Indeed, this style is often a reflection of who *they* are; often, those who prefer to be Macro-managed themselves will often manage in the same way. They assume you can do the job you were hired to do, and they expect you to do it.

The too-busy boss

This type of hands-off boss may want to provide guidance and support but can't seem to carve out the time. His plate is already overflowing, and you are just one more thing piled on it. This boss may be rushing from meeting to meeting, constantly crashing under deadlines, and just plain swamped. Perhaps these bosses don't delegate enough or perhaps their workload is too consuming, but they are hands off because they don't have the time to be hands on.

The apathetic boss

The apathetic boss is the true ghost and a true problem. This Ghost Boss not only doesn't show up, he doesn't really care. This no-boss boss has emotionally and intellectually checked out. Not only is this boss ghosting you, he also ghosts his own workload, often leaving it to you to pick up the slack. He provides zero leadership, avoids making any decisions, is rarely engaged physically or virtually, and may do the bare minimum at the last minute.

The technical expert

As we know, organizations tend to promote the technically stellar folks into management without any regard for their aptitude (or desire) to be a manager. Sadly, in many organizations, going into management is the only promotional path, so many technical experts are "forced" to take that path. This is the boss who has the time but not the inclination to manage you. It has nothing to do with you. These bosses are probably highly engaged in their work and in the organization, and they just don't want to manage you or anyone for that matter. They resist it because they don't enjoy it, they don't know how to do it, and, quite frankly, they don't want to do it.

Proven Strategies to Manage Up the Ghost Boss

1. **Do your job.**

   I know that sounds simplistic, but it can be easy to veer off course when someone isn't supervising or guiding you. Some people use it as a license to be lazy or work on other, more interesting (and enjoyable) projects, leaving the ones they were originally asked to do sitting on the shelf. At some point, somebody will notice. Just because your boss is a ghost doesn't mean you get to be one as well. As tempting as it may be, resist the urge to pick and choose your work or take long lunches every day. While a Ghost Boss provides you with great latitude to do other cool stuff, it doesn't get you off the hook for ensuring the stuff you were hired to do gets done. Always remember: people in your organization are watching. You can show up like a motivated, get-it-done person or you can show up like a slacker. Your professional reputation is at stake. How you respond to having a Ghost Boss can make or break your reputation. Slacker or leader. It's your choice.

2. **Step up. Be a self-sufficient self-starter.**
   Having a hands-off manager is a great opportunity to exercise your creativity, decision making, and entrepreneurialism. Stay one step ahead by staying attuned to the environment. If you know things need to get done, do them before being asked. Take extra initiative. Put on your big girl/big boy pants and make things happen.

3. **Get on the calendar.**
   Take the initiative to request meetings and get on your boss's calendar. Request short meetings and show up prepared. If your boss has an executive assistant, make him your best friend. Pay attention to your boss's schedule, and work your way into it.

Real-Life Story

Steve worked for an absentee boss who was constantly running from meeting to meeting with little time in between. However, Steve also noticed that on days when his boss had back-to-back meetings, his boss tended to eat lunch at his desk or stay later in the evening. Steve became king of the 10-minute pop-in meeting. He came to his boss prepared with his highest priority questions and needs. When he said, "I only need 10 minutes," he remained true to his word. Over time, he and his boss were able to develop a good shorthand, and Steve was able to get the guidance he needed to be successful.

4. **Build strong team relationships.**

   If you work on a team, do everything you can to support the team and encourage strong team relationships and communication. As a unit, you can turn yourselves into a self-directed team, which is a team that effectively combines their different skills and talents to work without the usual managerial supervision toward a common purpose or goal. As a team, you can support each other and provide cover for each other when you make decisions without the boss's help. In some ways, it provides cover for you, too.

Real-Life Story

A government client of ours called us to do some team building for them. As we discussed the scope of the project, it became clear that what they really wanted (and admitted) was to build the team to operate independently of their supervisor. The team's supervisor was a technically excellent performer but had no interest in being a manager. The team was in disarray. Nobody knew their roles or boundaries of authority. Projects were bottlenecked at the supervisor level, and team members lacked the guidance to set priorities. The organization decided that it was more important to keep this high performer happy than to hold him accountable to manage. While I'm not usually a fan of letting people off the hook for not doing a job that they are paid to do, in this case, the transparency of the whole situation made a huge difference. We worked with team and organizational leadership to help them create a self-directed team. We helped them carve out clear roles, responsibilities, and levels of empowerment. The team was empowered to make decisions and move projects forward without constant guidance from the supervisor. The supervisor put clear stakes in the ground around the types of decisions or projects that needed his review and the ones that didn't. The team also had an opportunity to clearly state their needs and wants from the manager. By having an open dialogue and setting clear expectations, the team was able to adapt to their Ghost Boss and perform at an elevated level.

5. **Become the go-to person.**

    Having an absentee boss is an excellent way to enhance and boost your professional reputation at your company. Because nature abhors a vacuum, be the one who helps find information, provides input, make decisions, and keeps projects moving in your boss's absence. Soon, people in the organization will notice. It's a great way to ensure that you are well positioned for internal promotion.

6. **Find a mentor.**

    If you are looking to your Ghost Boss to be a mentor or coach, keep looking. Instead of waiting for that ghost ship to come in, take the initiative and build other mentoring and coaching relationships in your organization and industry. Not only will this help you grow professionally, but it will also help you build a network of resources to help you solve problems and find answers.

Real-Life Story

Elizabeth was a relatively new program manager for a large marketing and events firm. She liked and respected her boss, Dan. He was smart, accomplished, and supportive – the few times a month that she could get his attention. While he was clearly engaged with his work, he wasn't good at providing timely feedback or guidance. He was a Macro-manager. Elizabeth was terrified of making a mistake and kept pestering Dan for help. During one meeting, Dan expressed frustration that he wasn't able to help Elizabeth more. Elizabeth suddenly realized that if she was going to succeed in this job (and she really wanted to) she was going to have to find another source of guidance. So, she did. She turned to her colleague, Mark, who had a few more years of experience in the field and in the organization, for help. It worked. Mark was more than happy to mentor and guide Elizabeth. Mark had actually noticed that Elizabeth was floundering a bit but didn't want to say anything. He was more than happy to help as long as Elizabeth was open to learning and feedback and was willing to take responsibility for her growth and development. Problem solved. Elizabeth soon flourished and even began mentoring others.

7. **Clarify boundaries and expectations.**

   Absentee bosses know they are absent. Remember, they either don't have time to manage or don't want to. So, take the time to learn where your boundaries of authority are and what input they want on projects and processes. Get specific answers to specific situations. For every project or responsibility, you should be clear about what you are and aren't allowed to do, decide, approve, purchase, forward, change, etc. If your boss is physically and virtually absent, then straight up ask her, "What do you want us to do when we can't find you or you are unavailable and a decision or action needs to happen?" Get clarity on the really important things.

8. **CYA.**

   Document everything. You may need it. With an absentee boss, it may be helpful to document assignments, due dates, requests, etc. Keep a good record of your work, your decisions, your questions, and how your time was spent so that potential misunderstandings are kept to a minimum. Let's say that your Ghost Boss failed to provide adequate input on an important project. If the project fails to meet expectations then at least you have documentation to prove that you did all that you could to get his input. P.S. CYA means "cover your ass."

9. **Keep communicating.**

   With an absentee boss, the onus is on you to initiate and manage communications. Resist the temptation to ghost yourself! Make sure you keep your boss regularly updated on projects. Request and set up regular meetings if possible. Make the meetings short and to the point. Come prepared with the topics, questions, and needs. Make sure you highlight important issues first. When you do need immediate attention make sure your boss knows it is a high priority and why it is important. Don't bury important stuff in an update memo. Yes, this is going to feel burdensome, but it needs to be done.

10. **To save or not to save?**

    In extreme cases, your Ghost Boss may be also ghosting on his job and responsibilities. If this is the case, you have some choices to make. You can either cover for your boss – doing his work and your work – or you can let him fail. If you are clearly doing your boss's work, then you have the choice to save him or not to save him.

If you choose **not** to save your boss, then make sure you have kept records that clearly indicate the failed task was 100 percent his responsibility. Just keep in mind that letting your boss fail may reflect poorly on you. Be sure you understand the political winds that are at play.

11. **Don't take it personally.**

Your boss's ghosting probably has nothing to do with you, so don't take it personally. Unless you are the only one she is avoiding – then it is you! In that case, you need to figure out what you are doing that is repelling your boss.

Strategy Recap

- Learn your boss's style so you can manage up accordingly.
- Step up to the plate. Be a self-starter.
- Get on your boss's calendar.
- Take some risks.
- Clarify expectations, boundaries, responsibilities, and decision making.
- Become the go-to person on your team.
- Document and keep track of what you are doing.
- Increase team communications and collaboration.
- Find other mentors to help guide your growth and development.

13

The Narcissist

"We have no patience with other people's vanity because it is offensive to our own."
—François de La Rochefoucauld

Real-Life Story

Charlie was excited about going to work for a newly elected government official. He knew that his new boss, David, had a reputation for having a very large ego; in fact, he was notorious for it. But he was also known to be charming, bold, and independent, someone who campaigned on making a difference. Charlie believed in David's mission and was honored to be a part of the team. That is until he actually started working there. As a former military person, Charlie was used to large egos and respect for authority and hierarchy. But what he witnessed working for David was something different altogether: "The office was chaos. Everybody ran around trying to appease David. There was no debate on policy or strategy. There was no speaking truth to power. It was all about stroking David's ego and puffing him up. Staff meetings were more about paying

(continued)

(continued)

tribute to David than about how we were going to accomplish our agenda. I've never seen anything like it. It literally made me sick. Public service is supposed to be about the public and not the publican. I left after six months."

One of the most dreaded and difficult bosses to deal with is the Narcissist. At first blush, the Narcissist often presents himself as charming, accomplished, charismatic, and confident, someone you'd love to follow. It's only after you are drawn into his orbit that you realize this person is a self-absorbed, power hungry, egotistical, attention-grabbing boss from hell. Narcissist Bosses have an exaggerated sense of their importance and their entitlement. They care more about their success and self-promotion than they do about the organization or their people. They have an unrelenting need for admiration, praise, and ego-stroking. They are quick to take credit for everything and even quicker to place blame on others. The Narcissist is incapable of self-reflection or acknowledging failures. They have an uncanny ability to be both bully and victim at the same time. Narcissists are not only difficult to manage, but they often create toxic work environments where subordinates scurry around the Narcissist trying to appease his overblown ego.

Signs of the Narcissist

Overblown ego

Narcissists have an exaggerated ego. They want – no, *need* – to be seen and viewed by others as the best, brightest, and most successful. They are guided by a vision of who they think they are and will fiercely protect that inflated image.

Power trippers

In the workplace, Narcissist Bosses thrive on their power. They enjoy being in a place of superiority and control. They need the people below them to know that they are in charge. Challenging their power is a dangerous affair. They won't like it or forget it. Ever.

Insatiable need for praise

In order for Narcissists to maintain their sense of self-worth, they need constant praise, applause, and adoration. They are a bottomless pit of need. They are peacocks whose feathers need to be incessantly fanned and praised.

Credit claimers

Often, Narcissist Bosses are reluctant to give praise or credit for fear of diminishing their own shine. They often "steal" the credit or overblow their contribution to team successes. Narcissists are exceptionally adept at positioning their leadership at the center of every positive accomplishment.

Blames and shames

While Narcissists are stingy with praise, they are usually quite generous with blame. One of the most disturbing aspects of working for Narcissists is their ability to blame and shame others. When things go awry, the Narcissist always points his fingers at others. Nothing is ever the Narcissist's fault.

Hostile to criticism

It's one thing to have a large enough ego where you are immune to criticism – not caring or heeding. But it's quite another to be actively hostile and adverse to it. When faced with criticism, the Narcissist hits back. Instead of reflecting on the feedback, the Narcissist attacks. As one famous US elected official is fond of saying, "If you hit me, I'll hit you back harder."

Shameless self-promoters

In order to protect and promote their larger-than-life egos, Narcissists are shameless self-promoters, name droppers, and self-aggrandizers. They love to talk about their superiority and tell tales of their successes. They drop the names of their powerful friends and affiliates and love to tell tales of how they defeated their enemies. Every story ends the same: they are the best and brightest.

Empathy? No. Exploitive? Yes.

Another classic sign of Narcissists is their utter lack of empathy for others. They just don't seem to be able to put themselves in another person's shoes or to understand the needs or feelings of others. This makes them predisposed to exploiting others. The truly narcissistic boss has no problem manipulating, bullying, or abusing his staff without proper recognition, compensation, or appreciation.

Scene stealers

It's probably no surprise that Narcissists frequently love to hear themselves talk. Being the center of attention is their favorite place to be. They often dominate meetings, conference calls, and other business gatherings. They will use these interactions to elevate themselves and their ideas, and all too often they resort to criticizing or diminishing the contributions of others.

Ethical ambiguity

One particularly disturbing aspect of the Narcissist Boss is his fluidity and capriciousness around ethics and truth. Narcissists often are unconcerned with facts and truth, readily bending them to fit their needs. Because they are so self-focused, they are more likely than other personality types to cross ethical boundaries in order to achieve the success to which they feel entitled. Many Narcissists truly believe that they are "above the law" and that rules don't apply to them. Plus, they often think that they are too smart to get caught.

Discover the Drivers: Understanding the Narcissist Boss

Understanding what drives Narcissist Bosses is not complicated. Just remember, you are dealing with people whose motivation, mental model, and framework for life is all about them:

- They are driven by ego.
- They are driven by their need to be venerated, adored, esteemed, and admired.
- They are driven by their need to be regarded and beheld as superior to others.
- They are driven by the need to protect their image and sense of self-worth.
- They are driven by the need for external validation.
- They are driven by the need to be seen as successful.

Proven Strategies to Manage Up the Narcissist

If you find yourself working for a Narcissist, you have a narrow set of options and strategies, most of which may not be appealing. Because Narcissists have such fragile egos and always put their needs in front of the needs of others, you may find that the best you can do is to protect yourself until you can get out. Thriving under a Narcissist is difficult, which means *surviving* a Narcissist is often the best option.

1. **Assess the upside: Is it worth it?**
   Narcissists often rise to the top of organizational life. They are often highly successful and influential people. Many Narcissists have built huge empires and have blazed trails in new industries. If you are able to navigate the difficulties of the Narcissist Boss, there may be positive payoffs in terms of career success, experience, and professional connections. Because Narcissists tend to be paranoid, if you prove yourself to be a loyal producer for them, they will often keep you along for the ride.

2. **Sycophants survive.**
   I hate that I just wrote that, because *Managing Up* is not supposed to be about brownnosing or sucking up. But in this one case, it actually is. Narcissists thrive on flattery. You don't have to be over the top, but complimenting and stroking the ego of the Narcissist will keep you in his good graces. It's what he wants and needs. You will feel less icky if you can find things that you truly do believe he does well. And please know that by doing this you will become part of the problem, so choose wisely.

3. **Respect, defer, and secure.**
   Narcissists are hypersensitive to feeling disrespected. Always make sure that you are demonstrating appropriate levels of respect and deferment to your Narcissist Boss. This is especially important when you need to present bad news or a differing point of view. Challenge her ideas carefully and thoughtfully. In these cases, how you deliver your messages becomes way more important than what you are delivering. Showing respect and a willingness to ultimately defer to your boss's authority

will increase her sense of security. An insecure Narcissist is prone to paranoia, suspicion, and volatility. Tread carefully and respectfully.

4. **Back away from the watercooler.**

Gossiping about Narcissists is a recipe for disaster. It will get back to them. Remember, narcissism breeds a culture of sycophantism, and that means whatever you say may be used against you by a colleague who is just trying to survive. If you need to vent (and you will) make sure you turn to outside friends and family. Or hire a therapist or coach who is paid to listen and keep your confidences.

5. **Learn what you can.**

Because Narcissists are often highly successful, you can actually learn quite a bit from them. Pay attention to what they do well and see what you can learn or emulate from them. Narcissists are usually more than happy to talk at length about their successes, experiences, and strategies. Ask their advice. Seek their counsel. Take as much good stuff as you can from the situation. This is actually a double bonus strategy because seeking their advice enriches your knowledge while simultaneously stroking their ego. It's a win-win.

6. **Appeal to their image.**

One way to challenge your Narcissist Boss is to appeal to his carefully crafted image. Psychologists tell us that true (in the clinical sense) Narcissists don't feel guilt, but they *might* feel shame. And they definitely feel fear about losing face or looking bad. Therefore, when trying to persuade, advise, or even challenge a Narcissist Boss, appeal to how his actions will look to the outside world. In other words, the "what will people think" is fertile territory for a status-conscious Narcissist. Offer neutral pros and cons for his decisions framed in terms of how these choices might impact his image, reputation, and career.

7. **Never make it about you.**

Since Narcissists are all about their own needs and wants, when you need or want something, make sure you frame it in terms of your boss's needs, not yours. For example, if you need some space or time out of the line of fire, frame it around their larger needs: "I really want project Y to be a home run for you. I'd like to be able to take a few days to reflect on our approach." Another important element to this strategy is to become really adept at managing your reactions to their ridiculousness. Resist appearing defensive, offended, frustrated, or disgusted. I know, but it works.

8. **Protect your image.**
   There will be times when your Narcissist Boss will throw you under the bus. Nothing sucks more, but it will happen. Narcissists are incapable of accepting blame. They consider that your job. When this happens, find ways to calmly set the record straight – and here is the tricky part – without making them wrong. Be neutral and nonconfrontational. Focus on the facts and not the assertions or distortions. Resist the urge to be snarky. Calmly state the facts, chain of events, or background information. This is best done in private with your boss. And please, try not to throw your colleagues under the bus.

9. **Protect your self-esteem.**
   Remember, it's not you, it's them. When working for a Narcissist, it is important that you don't take her behavior personally. Narcissists' demeaning and demanding behavior is who they are. Do whatever you can to compartmentalize their behavior. Protect your soul. Put on the golden psychic shield. And whatever you do, please don't subscribe to their formula for success. Don't let the narcissism rub off on you.

10. **Don't get sucked in.**
    Narcissists are expert charmers and manipulators. Don't let yourself get sucked into their manipulative ways. One day they love you, but when they are done with you, they will cut you out without a thought. Don't let yourself be manipulated or drawn too deeply into their web. Manage this relationship with your eyes wide open. Never forget: It's about them, not you.

11. **Get out.**
    Narcissism, like any other personality trait, is a spectrum. Mild or even medium-level narcissism might be manageable. But extreme narcissism is a completely different story. If you find yourself working for an extreme Narcissist, our best advice is to get out.

Real-Life Story

Sara found herself working for Adam – an extreme Narcissist. She did everything she could to make it work: "I took a position on Adam's policy team. I had known Adam casually as a coworker from another department. He was funny and a great writer. I thought I was making a good career move. But once in a position of authority he turned into a nightmare of narcissism. He was vicious, self-centered, envious, exploitative, rash, and completely lacking in empathy. It wasn't hard to figure out that I was now working for a Narcissist. I researched narcissism extensively. At first, I thought, I can handle this. I am a high-achiever type so I was confident that I could make this work. Initially, I thought compliance would work. Just do everything he asked, and he can't be unhappy. But with somebody who's exploitative, the more you do for him, the more he takes. Then I tried drawing lines with him, and that was absolutely horrible. He started screaming at me in front of other people when I drew a very, very appropriate boundary with him. I tried talking to his boss; that was a big mistake. When I tried to stop caring about how he treated me, he could tell. His reaction to the fact that I no longer cared was fascinating. He recognized very quickly that he had no more control over me. And then he just went on an absolute rampage to get rid of me. One strategy that someone else used on our team was complete self-abnegation. This person was completely nonthreatening at all times. Although he was a capable person, his professional reputation got damaged and he is not regarded as very talented or valuable by the organization. I knew I couldn't go down that route.

"My lightbulb moment came when I read this great analogy about Narcissists: You bring your cup to a well and then realize the water is poisoned. So, you think, what can I do? I can bring a different cup, and you try that, but the water is still poisoned. You take a different route to the well, but the water is still poisoned. You try all kinds of different ways to drink the water. But when the water is poisoned, the water is poisoned. It doesn't matter what cup you use or path you take; the water is still poisoned. My advice to anyone who's in a situation like this is to understand that you are in a no-win situation. Because, if you're like me and you to try to shine, he's just going to come after you. And if you're like my colleague and you try not to shine, you damage yourself professionally. Don't drink that water. Just get the hell out."

Strategy Recap

- Respect, defer, and secure. Demonstrate appropriate levels of respect.
- Flatter. Complimenting and stroking the ego of the Narcissist will keep you in his good graces.
- Do not gossip about the Narcissist. It *will* get back to her.
- Learn from them. Narcissists are often very successful, so try to learn something.
- Appeal to their image and protect yours.
- Don't get sucked in. Narcissist are expert manipulators. Try not to get sucked into their orbit.
- Remember, it is not about you; it is always about them.
- Assess the level of narcissism and be prepared to leave.

14

The Impulsive Boss

"Squirrel!"

—Dug the talking dog

Real-Life Story

Erik was the IT enterprise architect for a large law enforcement agency and reported directly to Hal, the chief information officer. "Hal was a diehard agency man. He loved the agency and loved the people. He was off the charts passionate. If you wanted any kind of internal sales pitch or rah-rah session, you'd call Hal. He was a whirlwind of ideas – and emotions. He was so passionate about the mission that it kind of blinded him to reality and made working for him really hard. He was constantly coming up with new ideas and initiatives – a total big-ideas guy. And this was not a big-ideas kind of organization, so we spent a lot of time chasing rainbows. He was famous for e-mailing us at 1:00 or 2:00 a.m. with his latest new ideas, just firing off these e-mails, like 'Tomorrow when you get in, we have to talk about...' Every time he had a new idea – he went all in. Of course, 99 percent of

(continued)

(*continued*)

the time, he came up with these grandiose ideas that just seemed unattainable to everybody. People would just roll their eyes and be like 'there he goes again.' His management style was to run from office to office, talking to people. 'Okay, a new issue has come out, we need to run to this office and talk to this other person. Okay, now we need to run to this office and tell them what we talked about in the other office' – and, of course, each meeting shifted the priorities. He was just simply all over the place. It wore me ragged. That's not the way I like to do things, and I couldn't keep up with him."

Is your boss a whirlwind of ideas? Constantly chasing every shiny object? Continually shifting priorities? Unable to stick to a plan? Frequently changes her mind or contradicts herself? Do his ideas, moods, and goals shift like the wind? Does she have a short and continually changing attention span? In short, is your boss like Dug the talking dog in the movie *Up*? "Squirrel!"

If you answered yes to any of the above, chances are you may have an Impulsive Boss on your hands.

For most people, Impulsive Bosses are difficult to navigate. The ever-changing directions, priorities, decisions, and moods can create chaos, uncertainty, and stress. Most human beings are wired to seek stability, certainty, and homeostasis, so working for a boss who creates chaos and uncertainty can be very challenging. There is a big difference between working for a boss who is open-minded, innovative, and risk taking, and one who is unfocused, unreliable, and imprudent. Common complaints we hear from our clients who work for impulsive bosses are:

- He constantly changes his mind. Our priorities are always shifting.
- Every time she goes to a conference she picks up a new pet project or strategy, which lasts about 48 hours, then we are off on another "new thing."
- My boss shoots from the hip. He makes decisions based on his gut and mood rather than logic or reason.

- We never know who our boss is going to be on any given day. Her moods change like the wind. Every mood brings a different set of priorities.
- It takes forever to finish a project. My boss constantly changes his mind on what he wants done.
- It feels like we are always reinventing the wheel, and we have a lot of "dead wheels" that never see the light of day.
- Everybody on the team is exhausted. We never know when an idea or direction is going to stick, so managing our time and workload is difficult.

Discover the Drivers: Understanding the Impulsive Boss

There are multiple reasons that your boss may be impulsive. Some are easily bored, some love change, some are desperately trying to make their mark, and some are, well, just incapable of sustained focus. A few common drivers of impulsive people include:

Oriented toward creativity, change, and innovation
Your boss may be wired to do new, different, and creative things. His expansive desire for change and innovation may cloud his ability to stick to any one change long enough to make it happen.

Easily bored

Your boss may get bored easily and may be energized by breaking out of routine projects, details, processes, etc. Easily bored people often seek new and different approaches and projects as a way to keep themselves energized and engaged.

Lack of experience
If your boss is new to the job or role, her impulsivity may stem from a lack of experience and a need to prove herself. Oftentimes people new to management want to quickly make an impact, to prove their mettle. So instead of steadily and strategically racking up wins and accomplishments they chase different, shiny objects in the hopes of proving themselves. ("Squirrel!")

Attention-deficit disorder (ADD)
Sometimes the lack of ability to focus, stay on task, finish projects, and utilize methodical decision making are symptoms of ADD, which may show up in the workplace as impulsivity.

Proven Strategies to Manage Up the Impulsive Boss

1. **Appreciate the intention, and reshape the energy.**
   Impulsive Bosses are often trying to make a positive impact. They probably want to do good and meaningful things; they just may not know how. Try to think of this behavior as a positive energy force that you have to learn to reshape into something useful. Think of it as a form of workplace jujitsu, where you take in your boss's energy and reshape it into something more useful, concentrated, and successful.

2. **Keep calm and carry on.**
   If your boss is a whirlwind of impulsivity, wait for the storm to pass. One of the most important things to understand about Impulsive Bosses is their facility to change their mind, and the high probability that they will. Therefore, don't get too caught up with every whim your Impulsive Boss throws out or, worse yet, her mood. Stay calm and don't panic – yet.

Real-Life Story

Donna worked for a very impulsive and mercurial boss at a West Coast landscaping company. She and her teammates created "weather forecasts" to assess their boss's moods so that everyone could be adequately prepared, or, in her words "dressed for the weather." "Calm and sunny" meant that all was good. "Wind speed of 10 mph" meant some new ideas were brewing, nothing too major, whereas "tropical storming warning, level 10" meant run and take cover! Donna and her colleagues looked out for each other. They all loved their jobs and worked together to manage their boss's whimsical nature.

---

3. **Be open-minded.**
   Don't become so resistant or annoyed by working for an Impulsive Boss that you close yourself off to innovation and good ideas. Would you rather work for some stuffy dinosaur who never innovates or changes? Try to get some perspective on how often your Impulsive Boss's shifts and whims pay off. If they rarely pay off,

fine. But if your boss has a track record of impulsiveness leading to some successes, then your best strategy may be to buckle up and go along for the ride. Who knows? Your Impulsive Boss may just strike gold.

4. **Mirror the mood.**

If your boss is excited about a new idea then try to mirror (and by mirror, I mean feign) some excitement yourself. Feigning excitement or interest in the idea doesn't mean you agree with it. "A satellite office on Mars? Why yes, that would be exciting!" "Reconstructing the entire human genome map? Why, yes, that would be a feather in our cap!" Resist the urge to immediately throw the proverbial wet blanket – that comes later. Instead, allow him to talk and explore the idea more fully. Ask a few probing questions about his idea: "How do you see this project unfolding? Where would we start? How much manpower would we need? Would we be able to get the budget for it?" And so on. This will not only (hopefully) help ground your boss in reality, but it will also give you an idea of what is important to him about this idea. Second, it positions you as a supporter and not a Debbie Downer. And last, if your boss is mercurial as well as impulsive, it helps to manage his mood. Oftentimes impulsive leaders react negatively when they perceive that others do not share their enthusiasm.

Conversely, when your impulsive and mercurial boss shows up moody and frustrated, show empathy. "Yes. It's too bad about the Mars project getting canned. That would have been cool." You can acknowledge and empathize without colluding. Mirroring the mood should be your default position. Then, you may deploy "reality check" strategies.

5. **Fill in the blanks. Offer a gentle reality check.**

After your Impulsive Boss impulses, then it is time to fill in the blanks. In other words, after you hear him or her out, come back with some concrete reality. It's best if you put some space between the initial impulse and your "plan" for activating. This is the time where you get to be the proverbial wet blanket. Come back to your boss with a gentle reality check. "So, I looked into the Mars project and discovered that at this time, the US government doesn't allow colonization on Mars – but we can get on the waiting list."

Provide real data on the project. And by "real" I do mean real. Present the data honestly with an open mind and as nonjudgmentally as possible. Remember, your boss wants to be effective. When possible, provide some options that may satisfy his impulse at some level: "Well, since we can't go to Mars, we could look to creating some virtual offices. My initial research indicates it would cost us XX dollars." Now, I know this is a silly example, but Impulsive Bosses are often creative, out-of-the-box thinking people, and their desire to do something new and different can be molded into more reasonable and doable goals. Try to present a clear direction with some options. If you have an opinion on the right course of action, try to nudge your boss that way: "So, I researched options for the human genome mapping technology. The best choices are Option A and Option B. I think Option B is the best because the price is similar, but it includes these additional options." Let me know if you want me to go ahead and purchase that system or if you prefer Option A." Yes, it is real work and yes, it might prove to be a waste of time, but you have to be the voice of reason without being the dream killer.

6. **Recap and keep track.**

   Shifting direction is what Impulsive Bosses do best, so they have a tendency to lose track of decisions, priorities, projects, and goals. Instead of expecting them to keep track, a great managing up strategy is to do it for them. Take responsibility for recapping conversations, project announcements, priorities, assignments, etc. Put them in writing. Recapping helps to focus, clarify, and confirm. It also provides cover. Get in the habit of sending off a quick e-mail to your Impulsive Boss after she shifts into some new territory. Something simple like, "Hey, boss, just to recap. As directed, we will research options for setting up a satellite office on Mars." Yes, it requires a little extra effort on your part, but what is your alternative? Spending countless hours stewing, stopping, and restarting? Managing up takes effort. Just remember: An ounce of prevention is worth a pound of cure.

7. **Triangulate for clarity.**

   In ordinary circumstances, triangulation is a bad communication practice. In normal circumstances, I would recommend going directly to the source of confusing information to clarify.

However, in the case of an Impulsive Boss, it can be helpful to triangulate information with your coworkers. One common impact of impulsive leadership is that communication and guidance tend to be a bit chaotic. People are told different things at different times. Make it a practice to check in with others in your department or team to triangulate what is happening. Share information and communicate frequently. This helps you and others understand if you're all being told the same thing.

8. **Create guardrails.**

It's okay to negotiate priorities. If your Impulsive Boss constantly changes direction and shifts goals and priorities, then you need to create some guardrails to keep yourself from crashing and burning. You do this by proactively discussing with him priorities and bandwidth. I know this is uncomfortable to some, but if you want to survive the whiplash, it must be done. Communicate frequently and forthrightly about priorities, schedules, must-haves, nice-to-haves, etc. Review, recap, and summarize your current projects, deadlines, and bandwidth. Put the onus on your boss to pick and stick.

9. **Hedge your bets.**

See if you can identify patterns to the shifting winds of your boss. What are the signs? Understanding the signs may allow you to hedge your bets and only invest fully in a new project when you're sure the priority will stick. This strategy worked well for Donna and her colleagues in the landscaping business discussed earlier. It was obvious that each time their boss went to an industry event or tradeshow he returned full of new ideas, priorities, and projects. It was also obvious that 95 percent of these new ideas, priorities, and projects fizzled out within two weeks. So, Donna and her colleagues learned to hedge their bets. They would invest only lightly in new ideas, just enough to be ready to move forward if, say, in a few days the new idea was still on their boss's radar.

10. **Be patient.**

Remember, if your boss is truly uncontrollably and inconvertibly impulsive, the odds are high that she will not see things through. She will get bored with the current position, pet project, or role and will (hopefully) move on. This uncontrolled impulsiveness also means Impulsive Bosses are more likely to make a large, expensive mistake that may end their reign of chaos.

Real-Life Story

At first Erik was freaked out and intimidated by Hal's leader-ship style. Then Erik decided that this was a challenge that he could manage. "I decided to go old-school and make this work. I decided to figure out what his currency was and work through it. I made it my job to put structure to our conversations. I started imposing meeting agendas on him. I would be like, 'Okay, here's the agenda, here's what we're going to discuss,' because other-wise, the sky was the limit with topics. At first it made me feel uncomfortable to be reeling him in during our meetings, but the more I did it, the easier it became. In fact, I think Hal learned to appreciate and expect me to do it! I also began to informally doc-ument and recap our conversations, meeting minutes, decisions, ideas, etc. through e-mail. Hal was big on e-mail, so this worked great. My e-mails were informal and simple – I'd just recap by say-ing things like 'Here's what I understood we discussed, and here's what we agreed upon in the meeting, here is what I think our pri-orities are, next steps, etc.' This was quite effective since it was very common for those who worked for Hal to leave meetings or conversations with completely different understandings over what we agreed upon. Taking meeting notes – so old-school, but so successful.

"Finally, I got into the habit of verbally recapping things in real time. Hal used to love to say, 'Are you picking up what I'm laying down?' I interpreted that to mean that I should reiterate to him what he just said so that he knew I got it. So, I would rephrase him and say things like 'Here's the situation, here's what you just told me, and here's what you want me to do. You want me to do X.' Once I learned that his impulsiveness was manageable, we developed a great working relationship. Even though I had to expend extra effort to manage him, it was worth it. At the end of the day, we were able to deliver some innovative solutions for the agency. It was a great learning experience."

Strategy Recap

- Try to see your boss's impulsivity as an energy that you can manage.
- Appreciate the intention. Reshape the energy.
- Wait for the storm to pass – don't respond to every whim and change.
- Try to mirror your boss's mood. Be excited about the things she is excited about, without going overboard.
- Don't be a wet blanket on your boss's excitement. Wait to bring in the facts.
- Create guardrails so you don't go off the road.
- Proactively discuss with your boss priorities and bandwidth.
- Try to identify patterns and signs for your boss's impulsivity, then hedge your bets accordingly.
- Recap, keep track, and triangulate with the team for clarity.

15

The Pushover

"It isn't the mountains ahead to climb that wear you out; it's the pebble in your shoe."
—Muhammad Ali

Real-Life Story

According to Michelle, her boss, Tom, was a total pushover and it was driving her and the rest of the team crazy. Tom was the executive director of a membership organization and by all accounts a really good person. "He is probably the nicest guy you ever want to meet. Everybody loves him. In some ways, he is perfect for his job because as head of a membership association, he does a great job building relationships and making our members feel important and valued. While I understand that being responsive to our members is a critical part of his job, I think he goes too far and bends too much. He seems incapable of taking a stand or sticking with a decision. For example, we may decide to go with X strategy, then he meets with a member who recommends Y strategy so we change. Then he meets with another member who wants X strategy and we go back. We are constantly shifting direction and changing decisions. It feels like a hamster wheel and it's frustrating everyone!"

Initially, the Pushover Boss may not seem so bad. In fact, he is probably pretty nice and easy going. He may let you do your own thing without too much resistance. You may think "Jackpot!" However, that first impression will fade fast as soon as that super nice, easy-going, Pushover Boss proves to be a real problem for you, your team, and the organization.

Pushover Bosses' inability to take a stand or to have the courage of their convictions can be extremely detrimental to organizational productivity and positivity. The Pushover's backbone is made of Jell-O. Pushovers can't stick to a decision. They allow employees to walk all over them, and they never have your back. Because the Pushover rarely holds employees accountable, the ones who suffer the most are the high-performers who quickly become frustrated with the lack of direction and the refusal to hold low-performing employees accountable.

Signs of the Pushover

Flip-flops and ducks decisions

The Pushover will often change her mind based on the last person she spoke with. Pushovers also may take agonizingly long to make decisions, grinding productivity to a halt. They just don't seem to have the guts to put a stake in the ground.

Sidesteps conflict

Pushover Bosses are notoriously conflict averse. They flee from conflict and confrontation, which makes it difficult to advance projects that incorporate diverse ideas. Healthy conflict and debate are important elements for high-performing teams, so having a Pushover as a leader prevents teams from achieving their true potential.

Avoids accountability

Because Pushovers are conflict adverse, they are incapable of holding employees accountable for performance. This is a major problem for morale. Refusal to address low-performing or problem employees is guaranteed to make hardworking employees angry, frustrated, and demoralized.

Clings to the status quo

Pushovers don't lead; they just go with the flow. They are on autopilot and prefer to stay in their comfort zone. This means they are willing to accept mediocre results instead of going out on a limb to achieve greatness. If you are a person who wants to perform at a higher level, this will be a problem for you.

Can't say no

Just as Pushovers allow employees to walk all over them, they also can't say no to or push back against higher ups. In essence, they are the quintessential yes-man. Anyone who has ever worked for a yes-man knows that his inability to negotiate or push back on requests from bosses or peers means that your workload will probably overwhelm you and your team's bandwidth and resources.

Fears feedback

Your Pushover Boss will probably only give your performance positive commentary. While this may feel good at first, please know it probably is only half sincere and will ultimately be detrimental to your professional growth and development. Not having a boss who is willing to give you honest feedback – both positive and constructive – prevents you from learning and growing.

Abandons advocacy

One of the biggest dangers of Pushover Bosses is their inability to advocate for you or your team. Don't expect Pushovers to stand up for you or have your back during conflict or difficult times. Their inability to stand up to others means that they are much more likely to drop you in the fire like a hot potato or even throw you under the bus.

Discover the Drivers: Understanding the Pushover

People who work for a Pushover report feeling angry, frustrated, annoyed, and dispirited. While those are absolutely valid emotional reactions to this kind of boss, it is important to manage those emotions so that you can be more effective in your managing-up strategies. While there isn't much chance that your Pushover Boss will suddenly grow a backbone, it is helpful to understand what may be going on for her. The primary underlying emotional drivers of the Pushover Boss are often fear, insecurity, inexperience, and a need to please everyone.

People pleasers

Pushovers are often people pleasers. They go out of their way to please everyone, saying yes to everything and never doing anything that will cause even a whiff of conflict. But we all know you can't please everyone in life, and certainly not in the workplace.

Fearful and insecure

Pushover Bosses operate from a place of fear. They fear conflict. They fear disappointing people. They fear making a mistake. They fear being the bad guy. They fear not being liked. They fear everything. Pushovers lack confidence, courage, and conviction. Another common trait among Pushovers is their insecurity. They may lack confidence in their ability to make decisions, achieve results, and take risks. They lack courage to stand up for themselves (and their employees). For some reason, either by nature or nurture, they are not capable of exhibiting or demonstrating much conviction.

Inexperienced

Sometimes the problem is a lack of experience. Newly minted managers are often timid about using their authority, so they may be reluctant to take the lead. This may be a result of being new to the role, the organization, or the team. This often shows up when a team member is suddenly put in charge of the team. They may be reluctant to "boss their friends around" and may not understand how to navigate in their newly elevated role. Their discomfort with their new power causes them to shrink instead of rise.

Real-Life Story

In a recent workshop, a participant named Anna confessed to being a "recovering" Pushover Boss. We were all ears. Here is what she said: "I became a manager at XX organization after having just left a managerial position in another company where I had been micromanaged to within an inch of my life. My former boss was hyper-controlling and critical. Nothing was ever good enough for him. Even though I was a manager, I wasn't allowed to make decisions or lead my team without clearing everything with him first. I guess I didn't realize how damaged I was when I came here. I think I had workplace PTSD! For the first couple of months, I was terrified to make a decision or make a mistake. I was unsure about the organizational culture or what my new boss expected of me. I tried so hard not to be the horror show that was my former boss that I let my new team walk all over me. I'm totally embarrassed to admit it, but I had lost all my confidence and backbone. Luckily, most of my team was encouraging and supportive of my learning curve. It took about six months, but I am pleased to say I think I've grown about 75 percent of my backbone back. I'm not quite where I want to be, but I am trying hard to get there."

While Anna's situation is probably more atypical, it does show that a Pushover may be able to grow the confidence, experience, and courage needed to be effective, at least when the pushover is inexperienced or new to the role of manager. Keep your mind open to that possibility, but don't put all your eggs in that basket.

Proven Strategies to Manage Up the Pushover

1. **Get to know them.**
   As with the case of Anna's story, if you take the time to get to know Pushovers you may learn more about what is driving their behavior. Knowing their history, experience, and personality will help you determine how best to navigate them. If they lack confidence because they are new managers, be sure to encourage and support them when they make good decisions. If they are insecure because they are new to the organization, help them understand how things work at your company.

2. **Encourage, support, and respect.**
   Transcend your frustration and be actively supportive and encouraging. The Pushover Boss is overly susceptible to the opinions of others, so make sure that your opinion is strongly and consistently in the mix. Provide good data whenever possible to help support your boss's decision making. Arm him with good information. Sure, your pushover boss will probably disappoint you time after time, but at least you will be in the mix. Hone your influence and persuasion skills.

3. **Seek constructive feedback elsewhere.**

The Pushover is not going to give you any useful or constructive feedback. Look to other high-performing colleagues or mentors to help with your professional growth and development.

4. **Fill the vacuum.**

A Pushover Boss leaves a power vacuum. Look for ways to fill it (using your powers for good, of course). Take some calculated risks. Look for opportunities to make decisions. Stay attuned to organizational rhythms and conditions. Look for ways to proactively solve organizational problems and fill needs. Connect with influencers in other departments and find subtle ways to improve your group's performance.

5. **Be proactive about being proactive.**

Keep your boss apprised of your work. Let your boss know when you are taking initiative. Arm her with as much knowledge as possible. Give her the what *and* the why. Always make sure she understands the *why* of what you and the team are doing. The more she clearly understands the rationale, context, and benefits of your projects, goals, and/or processes, you may be able to stave off some of her waffling.

6. **Make your boss look good.**

As much as you may hate this strategy, please remember: fearful people fear losing face, respect, friends, etc. Do what you can to make your boss look good. The worst thing you can do to an insecure boss is make him feel even more insecure.

7. **Circumvent with caution.**

Another strategy to managing Pushover Bosses is to go around them and over their head in an effort to get guidance or decisions from the powers above them. This can work, but only if the conditions are right. You must pay attention to the politics at play. If the culture is one that is accepting and embracing of the pushover boss – after all, she might be a great yes-man – then this may not be a good option. If your Pushover has a great relationship with her boss or has powerful political protection, then abort the mission.

If, however, your Pushover is an anomaly and the culture is competitive and hard-driving, then you might consider building a relationship with your boss's boss. Create opportunities to share ideas, pitch projects, and learn about his goals. Find ways to demonstrate your enthusiasm and desire to contribute to organizational success – but without throwing your boss under the bus. This kind of influencing up takes finesse, tact, and time. Be careful, cautious, and thoughtful.

8. **Focus on your work.**

One of the most disheartening things about working for a Pushover is that while you are working conscientiously and diligently, others get away with murder. Loafers, slackers, and poor performers are rampant in teams led by pushovers. This sucks. It is totally unfair, I agree. But you *cannot* focus on other people. I know, I know, it's not fair. But remember, your Pushover Boss is *never* going to hold them accountable, so let it go. Don't waste your energy or brainpower feeling bitter and vengeful. Focus on doing the best job you can. Focus on advancing your career. Focus on achieving positive results for you and the organization. People will notice.

Real-Life Story

Michelle decided that instead of being frustrated by Tom, she was going to help him. She knew that Tom hated conflict and was very reluctant to say no to members, so she and the team began bolstering his decisions with data. They gave him solid information that supported the choices the organization made – so when members began suggesting alternative strategies, Tom had the data that supported the chosen strategy. She also suggested that before Tom made an organizational decision, he meet with several members at the same time – members who usually had different perspectives – and use these meetings to come to a consensus on decisions. This way, Tom would get allies and backing before the decisions were made and he wouldn't have to be the "bad guy." Michelle knew that Tom was never going to grow a backbone, so she helped him develop an external and internal support structure. "While I can't say that he has become a strong

(continued)

(continued)

leader, I can say that the strategies are helping us stay focused a bit more. The decision-making process takes longer, but at least he is doing a much better job of sticking with the decisions that are made!"

Strategy Recap

- Get to know the Pushover. Learn about his experiences, fears, and ambitions.
- Look to other high-performers for constructive feedback, challenging projects, and developmental opportunities.
- Keep your boss apprised of your projects and processes and their impact.
- Fill the power vacuum with honorable intentions.
- Encourage, support, and respect your boss. Make her look good to avoid heightening her fear and insecurity.
- Circumvent with caution. Pay attention to the politics at play before you attempt to go around your boss to her boss.
- Focus on your work and ignore the slackers around you.

16

The BFF Boss

"When a man's best friend is his dog, that dog has a problem."

—Edward Abbey

Real-Life Story

Lisa is a friendly person who has always done well making work friends. She was excited about her new job and appreciated that her new boss, Wendy, was so friendly. Wendy really seemed to care about her and was actively seeking to get to know her. At first Lisa was happy about the friendship she was building with her new boss. In no time, she and Wendy were having lunch together almost daily and often enjoyed after-work drinks. They texted each other frequently over the weekend and often met up for movies, shopping, and other weekend activities. Lisa was flattered that Wendy was so open about her life and confided in Lisa about her personal and professional life. Wendy would often call Lisa into her office to complain, confide, and grouse, always expecting Lisa to be there as a friend.

(continued)

(continued)

Then suddenly, Lisa started to feel uncomfortable. Her boss was sharing too much and expecting too much. Her boss was starting to feel too needy. At the same time, Lisa started to hear snide remarks from her colleagues about her relationship with Wendy. Things like, "Of course you got that project. You're Wendy's favorite." Lisa also noticed that her peers were starting to ice her out a little bit. "I'd walk into the break room and all the conversation would stop. People would say hello to me, but it was clear that the conversation definitely changed once I was in the room."

Lisa had a problem and she knew it. She had unwittingly become her boss's BFF. Yikes!

Ahhh, the allure of the "friend boss." It seems like such a good idea at the time. We all want our bosses to care about us. We all want to have friendly relations with our boss. Who doesn't want to feel cared about, supported, and liked at work? Isn't it better to have a friendly boss than an unfriendly boss? What could go wrong?

Plenty. There is a big difference between being *friendly* with your boss and being *friends* with your boss. There is a difference between being work friends and personal friends. And there is a **huge** difference between being friends and being *best* friends. The former can help you succeed, the latter can be a recipe fraught with potential career land mines. Here are some things to consider before jumping on that BFF train with your boss.

Remember that your boss is your boss *first* and your friend *second*. He doesn't love you unconditionally – as a friend would. He loves you *conditionally* – as long as you perform and give him what he wants or needs. Let's say you are great friends with your boss, then comes a time when he has to give you a negative performance review or sharp-edged criticism. Chances are you will feel whiplashed, hurt, and confused. "But I thought we were friends!"

I am not saying don't be friends with your boss. I am saying be careful that your work friendship doesn't cross the line into the overly personal zone. It's tricky to navigate and even harder to identify.

It can be tough to know where that line is. Some people need and want a larger zone of personal space, others revel in creating strong friendships with their boss. If it is mutual, if you want to be best friends with your boss, just be aware that it may create difficulties for you down the road. Be careful about how much you reveal about your private life and how much you start to learn about your boss's private life. And never forget that she is first and foremost your boss. When your boss wants more of a friendship than you are comfortable with then you have to carefully draw your boundaries. Bosses who conflate work friendships with personal friendships are putting themselves and you in a situation that could backfire on you, your reputation, your heart, and your career.

The BFF Boss Danger Zone

There are several major drawbacks of allowing yourself to be drawn into being your boss's best friend.

Lack of feedback

Feedback is notoriously difficult to give and to receive. Bosses are no exception. In fact, most cases of workplace distress result from managers not giving timely and appropriate feedback. A BFF Boss will only exasperate this common condition. The bottom line is most friends don't give friends honest feedback. If your boss is your BFF, he may be reluctant to give you consistent and helpful feedback. This will stunt your growth and development. On the flip side, if your boss does give you feedback, you may take it too personally. Hearing feedback from anyone is tough, but toss a friendship into the mix and the potential for awkwardness and hurt feelings skyrockets.

Peer backlash

Another potential quagmire with the BFF Boss is the backlash you are apt to receive (overtly or covertly) from your peers. When people suspect you and the boss are BFFs they will treat you differently. They may be suspicious of you, they may be jealous of you, they may overlook your great work and attribute your success to being the boss's pet. In short, they will stop trusting you. They may even gossip about your friendship to others outside the department, which can have an impact on your standing with the rest of the organization.

Career stagnation and bad blood

Nobody wants to lose their best friend. Including your boss. When your boss is your best friend, she may resist your leaving. BFF Bosses may not provide opportunities for your advancement out of fear of losing you. They also may be reluctant to let you go because you know too many secrets about them. If your boss has over-shared with you, she may worry about you revealing her skeletons. Conversely, you may be hesitant to leave them when you find other opportunities. Your reluctance to hurt your boss's feelings may keep you in a job longer than is good for you.

Real-Life Story

John had grown unhappy in his job but he was afraid to tell his "buddy" boss. When he finally did leave, his boss was hurt that John hadn't told him that he was unhappy. The boss took it very personally and began badmouthing John in the organization and industry, labeling John as a flake and a traitor. John learned a hard lesson and has vowed to never make that mistake again.

Hoisted by your own petard

Over-sharing personal details about your life may come back to bite you. Remember, no secret is ever safe. In *Hamlet*, Shakespeare coined the expression "to be hoisted by your own petard" which means "to cause the bomb maker to be blown up with his own bomb." In this instance, your secrets may turn out to be your bombs. Remember, there are some things that you should **never ever** share with your boss.

Real-Life Story

Candace over-shared her weekend merriments on a regular basis. Candace and her boss regularly laughed about Candace's penchant for being "over-served" and the exploits that ensued. In fairness to Candace, she often exaggerated the stories to make her boss laugh. She loved that he loved her stories and he would often say, "Ah, to be young again..." While Candace thought that they were bonding as friends (and they may well have been), she didn't realize that these stories were affecting the way her boss viewed her as a professional. This came to light when Candace was passed over multiple times for promotions. When asked why, her boss told her that while he adored her as a person, he thought she was still too immature for a promotion and pointed to her weekend stories as an example. Candace was hoisted by her own petard.

Proven Strategies to Manage Up the BFF Boss

1. **Be friendly, but not best friends.**
   It's a fine line that you'll have to walk with the boss who wants to be BFFs. You *do* want to be friendly. You *do* want to engage in friendly conversation and show interest in her life. You *do* want to engage in friendly chit-chat and accept the occasional invitation to lunch, coffee, drinks, etc. You *don't* want to give the BFF Boss the total cold shoulder. While getting to know your boss as a person (and vice versa) will help build trust, never forget that it's a slippery slope.

2. **Draw boundaries. Share some, hide some.**
   Getting to know your boss as a person (and vice versa) can and will help build trust. And if you have a BFF Boss, he probably needs more relational activity to build trust with you. That's fine. Just be careful not to over-share. When we become friends with people we tend to let down our guard and divulge. In this case, you may find yourself divulging things at work you never would have before. There is a big difference between: "We had a great weekend. We went to that new bistro. It was packed, so we had to wait at the bar for about an hour for a table. But the place was great so it was worth the wait." And: "We had a great weekend. We went to that new bistro. It was packed, so we had to wait at the bar for about an hour for a table. By the time they sat us we were hammered! My husband had to leave in the middle of dinner to throw up. Our waitress was a total cow, so we stiffed her.

Then she confronted us outside the restaurant and we got into a screaming match. It was pretty funny." The first is light, informational, and friendly. The second is over-sharing and a little too illuminating. Which one might have an impact on your chances of promotion?

3. **Get busy.**

   While I do think you should accept the occasional invitation to socialize with your boss, you want to limit this so as to avoid crossing the threshold from friendly to BFF. If your boss constantly asks you to go to lunch, have coffee, do happy hour, hang out, or talk on the weekends, then you need to get busy with other commitments, real or imagined. "Drinks? I'd love to. But I have a yoga class. Lunch? Drat. I already promised I'd call my sister during my lunch break. Dinner? Sounds great, but I have to pick up the kids." Make yourself unavailable. Decline with kindness.

4. **Include others.**

   If you have a boss who wants to be friends, try to include others in that friendship. This will help both deflect some of the boss's neediness and also help reinforce relationships with your peers. It will cut down on the impression that you and your boss share a special bond. Including others in the happy hours and lunches should diminish the chances of peer backlash or gossip.

5. **Mind the social media.**

   Be careful about including your boss in your social media outlets. Facebook, Instagram, Twitter, and the like are potential career land mines. Weigh the pros and cons carefully before accepting the invitation from your boss to follow your feed. Control the access that your boss has to your site. Or better yet, let your boss know that you would prefer to connect with him on LinkedIn. Do what you can to keep your social media connections with your boss professional and not personal.

6. **Don't gossip. Don't complain.**

   When you are with the BFF Boss, avoid gossiping about others – even if the boss starts it – at all costs. Don't weigh in. While this is good advice in general – for any type of boss – it is even more critical for the BFF Boss. Gossiping with this boss will absolutely come back to haunt you. Don't do it. Ever. Also, be careful about complaining and venting with your BFF Boss. While it may seem like a safe space, it isn't. This person has authority over you. Like the over-share, everything you say will start to infiltrate and inform your boss's perception of you.

Real-Life Story

I once hired a friend to work on an important client project. She was a real pro, and I was excited to have her on the project. Now, when we were friends, we would occasionally vent about our difficult clients. We were peers, and it was nice to share our frustrations. But now, she was venting and complaining to me about my client – her job! Needless to say, I never hired her again.

7. **Don't flaunt the friendship.**
   Even if you haven't entered the danger zone of the BFF Boss, be sure not to overplay or flaunt your friendship with your boss. Keep it low key. Also, be on the lookout for real or perceived special treatment. Periodically look around and see if you are in fact getting special treatment. Are you getting all the plum assignments? Do you get special treatment for time off or other requests? Does your boss defer more to you than others in meetings? Are you and your boss sharing too many inside jokes in front of others? Monitor both the reality and the perception. If you think you might be getting special treatment, encourage your boss to give others more opportunities, be careful to not ask for special favors, and be inclusive yourself in meetings.
8. **Proactively ask for feedback.**
   One of the dangers of the BFF Boss is the lack of constructive feedback. As we discussed earlier, giving honest feedback to friends is a sensitive and difficult conversation. Make sure you proactively ask and receive feedback. You'll have to lead the conversation. Make it easy for your boss to tell you the truth. Ask your boss pointed questions on specific projects, such as "What could I do more of, less of, or differently next time?" That's a great way to get the ball rolling on constructive feedback.

9. **Have a conversation.**

It is possible to discuss friendship boundaries with your boss. This is a delicate conversation where you have to strike a balance between maintaining good relations and drawing boundaries. This conversation works best and is easiest when your friend or your peer *becomes* your boss. If this is the situation, I recommend having that conversation openly and quickly. Openly discuss the fact that your friendship *will* and *should* change now that she is your boss. Reinforce your fondness, support, and goodwill for this person, while having an honest discussion about the evolving relationship.

Real-Life Story

Lisa thought long and hard about her options. She could either have a direct conversation with Wendy about the impact of their friendship or she could slowly start to disentangle herself. She chose the latter. She was afraid that a direct conversation would embarrass Wendy and would ultimately backfire as she suspected Wendy would feel rejected. So Lisa decided to slowly rip off the Band-Aid. She gradually started to dial back the relationship and wean Wendy off her neediness. While remaining friendly and caring at work, she limited her time spent kvetching in Wendy's office. If Wendy wanted to gossip about one of their colleagues, Lisa would say something like, "Oh, I've never noticed that about him" and change the subject. She started inviting others to join them for lunch and happy hour. She started getting busier on the weekends. Instead of returning Wendy's non-work-related texts immediately, Lisa would wait a few hours before replying with a simple LOL or other appropriate emoticon. It was a delicate balancing act, but Lisa managed to pull it off. Soon, she was enjoying better relationships with her colleagues, and, while she was still friendly with Wendy, she had extricated herself from the BFF trap.

Strategy Recap

- Be friendly, but not best friends.
- Share some and save some. Beware the over-share (on either side). Draw and maintain boundaries.
- Get busy. Don't accept every invitation.
- Include others in your friendship outings.
- Mind your social media connections and sharing.
- Don't flaunt the friendship.
- Proactively ask for feedback.
- Have the conversation when your friend becomes the boss.

17

The Workaholic

"There's no crying in baseball!"

—Jimmy Dugan, *A League of Their Own*

Real-Life Story

After a bad experience in a previous job, Josephine promised herself that she was not going to sacrifice her personal life ever again. That was until she took a position working for Heidi, a senior executive in the federal government. Heidi was a force of nature. She was brilliant, dedicated, and hard-charging (yes, they exist in the government!). Heidi was on a mission and expected those around her to share her passion and her around-the-clock work mentality. While Josephine deeply wanted to protect her work-life balance, she also knew that working for Heidi at this point in her career could be a huge bonus. While she was inspired by Heidi's mission and wanted to make the most of this opportunity, Josephine wasn't sure she was game for the 24/7 challenge ahead.

Ah, the Workaholic Boss. He arrives before you do and is always there later than you. She puts in 12-hour days, every day. He works every weekend and late into the night. She sends e-mails and texts at all hours, including on the weekends. He can't seem to get enough of work. She thinks nothing of assigning you projects at 5 p.m. that are due the next morning. He never takes vacations. She piles on work without stopping to consider your bandwidth. Everybody is afraid to leave the office before he does. You find yourself glued to your phone, reluctant to make evening or weekend social plans. You wonder, does she have a life? You worry that you are losing yours.

Workaholic Bosses are everywhere. They "live to work" and often expect (and usually) favor those who share their appetite and zeal for this "all-in" work mentality.

Here's the potential good news: Working for highly motivated, task-oriented, always "on" Workaholics can be a career booster. If your boss is a fast-moving, high-achieving mover and shaker, and if you are ready, willing, and able to join that train, then you may find your career on the fast track. This "live to work" mentality can be exhilarating and exciting. You can learn a lot and give your career a boost.

The not-so-good news, however, is that working for a Workaholic can be extremely stressful, overly consuming, and downright damaging to your physical, mental, and emotional health. If you are a person who values a work-life balance and wants or needs a firm separation between work and life, then the Workaholic Boss may not be your cup of tea. You may find yourself burned out, stressed out, frustrated, overwhelmed, and depressed.

Discovering the Drivers: Understanding the Workaholic Boss

The first step to surviving (or thriving) with a Workaholic Boss is to understand what may be driving them. Taking a moment to understand what is driving your boss can help you choose the right strategies, and a little bit of empathy will help you clarify the right approach to take. Common drivers of workaholics include:

Pressure from above
What is the pressure being put on your boss? What is the organizational culture? Is he facing unreasonable deadlines? Is she working crazy hours because she *wants* to or *has* to?

Industry norms

What type of work approach is common in this industry? Is your boss the norm for someone in his position or is he more hard-driving than others with similar positions within the industry?

Organizational status

What's happening in your organization? Are you working for a start-up? Is your company trying to regain footing or a competitive advantage? Is your company going through large-scale change, restructuring, or ramping up to be more competitive?

Personal passion

Is your boss just simply passionate about what she does? Does she live-to-work because she simply loves what she does and finds work rewarding and fulfilling?

Ambition and/or ego

Does your boss have a substantial desire to succeed? To win? To climb the corporate ladder? Is your boss's sense of identity tied up with whether he is seen as successful?

Work *is* their life

Sometimes Workaholics simply have nothing to go home to. Does your boss have a fulfilling personal life? Has your boss experienced personal loss or other personal challenges that have driven her to put all her energy and focus on work?

Proven Strategies to Manage Up the Workaholic Boss

1. **Isolate the issue.**
   Isolate the issue and assess the situation. If you are having trouble managing your Workaholic Boss it's helpful to pinpoint what is most problematic for you: Is it the pace of the workload? The amount of work on your plate? The level of incessant urgency? The number of hours required or expected? The after-hours expectations? Whatever it is, make sure you are clear about where you are struggling.

2. **Know before you go.**
   This is actually a pre-strategy. If you are a nine-to-fiver and work-life balance is important to you, then it is your responsibility to know this *before* you go to work for a Workaholic

Boss or *before* you enter a workaholic culture or profession. It is your responsibility to know the work level expectations before you take that job. If you are suddenly surprised by your Workaholic Boss's expectations of you, then you didn't do your homework during your interview. Workaholics aren't shy about their proclivities. In fact, they usually wear their workaholism like a badge of honor. A simple question like, "What does it take to be successful here?" will usually do the trick. When your prospective boss says something like: "People who succeed here work hard and are dedicated to achieving results" it's code for "This ain't no nine-to-five gig." So if you didn't ask about expectations, shame on you. If you asked, but didn't "hear" the answer, double shame on you.

It is equally important to have a realistic understanding of the profession, the industry, the organizational culture of the particular business. There are some industries and professions where a 50–60 hour work week is not only the norm but is often considered the *minimum* level of effort required and expected. Professional services like consulting, accounting, law firms, media, advertising, investment banking, technology, and start-up endeavors are all notorious for long working hours. If you choose to work in one of these fields or organizations, be prepared to put in the hours. Take Paul's case, in the following example.

Real-Life Story

Paul was a first-year associate at a large law firm in Georgia. On the Wednesday before Thanksgiving, a partner assigned him to write a brief. Paul assumed that he would start it on Monday morning; after all, this partner couldn't possibly expect Paul to work over the Thanksgiving weekend. You can guess how the story goes. The partner e-mailed Paul midday on Friday and asked to see the rough draft. Paul hadn't even started it yet. In fact, Paul didn't even check his e-mail until Sunday afternoon. The ensuing Monday morning conversation didn't go well for Paul. According to Paul: "This was my own personal 'come-to-Jesus' moment. Although I knew that the legal profession demanded extraordinary effort, it never felt real to me until that moment. I quickly realized that if I wanted to succeed in this profession and at this firm (and I did) then I had to ramp up my work habits to meet the firm's expectations."

3. **Get sh*t done.**

   Usually, Workaholic Bosses are impressed by results. Lots of results. Put your productivity into overdrive, every day. That means no Internet surfing, no Candy Crush, no Facebook, Twitter, Snapchat, or Instagram during work hours. Your goal is to maximize your productivity through exceptional time management, focus, and goal setting. Anybody can log in hours and keep busy during the work day, but it takes real focus and commitment to stay actively productive throughout the day. Study after study shows that most office workers are actually only truly productive for about three to four hours a day. Thriving under a Workaholic Boss while maintaining a work-life balance requires bringing your A game each and every day. It's hard for a Workaholic Boss to dismiss your work habits if you consistently produce outstanding results and meet all your obligations.

4. **Prioritize your productivity.**

   Make sure you are working on the right things – the important things – first. Being productive is a good thing. Being productive on priority projects is a greater thing. Don't procrastinate on priority projects. Tackle the tough stuff first. If you consistently deliver high-quality results on priority projects, your Workaholic Boss may never even notice that you aren't burning the midnight oil.

5. **Know what the Workaholic wants.**

   That said, some Workaholics prize "butts in seats" as much as or more than results. Take Paige's story: She was hired as the VP of membership and business development for her city's Chamber of Commerce. Paige excelled at this job. In fact, she was born to do this job. It was totally in her sweet spot, and within the first few months she had far exceeded all the revenue and program goals that had been set for her. She was thrilled. The problem?

Robert, the CEO, was a Workaholic, the type that regularly put in 12-hour days, and he expected his staff to do the same, regardless of results. Paige noticed that nobody left the office until Robert did (which was usually around 8:00 p.m.), regardless of whether they were actively working. In fact, most of them just sat at their desks for appearance's sake. Their Workaholic Boss valued *input* over *output*. Robert prized hours worked over results attained. While Paige's output – her results – were remarkable, she quickly learned that in order to be successful with Robert, she would have to "play the desk game." She weighed the pros and cons and decided that her talents were better suited for a boss who respected and valued results rather than hours. She left after a year and never looked back. Figure out which type of Workaholic Boss you have – results or hours – and decide for yourself if it's worth it.

6. **Align your boundaries with their expectations.**
   It's okay to set boundaries with your Workaholic Boss. Don't be passive-aggressive. Verbalize your needs while still expressing dedication to the job and a desire to meet your boss's expectations. Instead of approaching it this way, "I don't work past 5 p.m.," try "I want to be as productive as possible during work hours because it is difficult for me to respond to e-mails after 6 p.m. due to my child-care responsibilities." Discuss with your boss her expectations about work hours. Negotiate your needs with these expectations and suggest solutions that work for both of you. It's not an easy conversation, but if you do it in the spirit of trying to adapt to and meet her needs, you might find a compromise that works for both of you.

Real-Life Story

Janet loved her job as a financial analyst. But since her twins were born, she was having trouble keeping pace with her Workaholic Boss, Darren. The pressure was piling up and Janet was at her wit's end. She was afraid that if she complained, she would be seen as less committed than her peers and her career would stall.

"Out of desperation, I finally decided I had no choice but to raise the issue with my boss," she said. "I scheduled a meeting and just laid it out as honestly and constructively as I could. I told Darren that I loved my work and my job, and that while I wanted to be available to him and the team as much as possible, the truth was that I was just stretched too thin and I feared that this pace was impacting the quality of my work. I'd be lying if I didn't say a flash of disenchantment crossed Darren's face. But I presented my case as positively as possible. I made suggestions on how I could adjust my schedule without losing steam. Even though I was no longer able to work late into the evening, I offered to check my e-mails after the twins went down to make sure I was on top of the latest developments and provide time-sensitive input on projects." Janet and Darren were able to negotiate expectations and boundaries. While Janet still feels the pressure to perform, the strategies and boundaries she set with Darren have helped her create the balance that she needs and still be a highly valued employee.

7. **Check your assumptions.**

   Are you sure your Workaholic Boss expects you to answer her weekend and evening e-mails? Many workaholic bosses simply fire off e-mails as they are plowing through their to-do lists and cleaning out their inbox. Have a conversation with your boss about her expectations. Create an agreement about reaching you after hours, both in terms of how and under what circumstances. For example, my staff knows that they can ignore my weekend e-mails until Monday, but if I text them over the weekend, it means that I really need a piece of information or action sooner rather than later. That means if they get a text from me they know to at least provide an acknowledgment of my query. Workaholics will feel less anxious if they know that when they really need you, they can access you.

8. **Shift and align your work hours.**

   You may prefer working 7 a.m. to 4 p.m., but if your Workaholic Boss works 8 to 6, you may consider shifting if you can. You'd be amazed at the impact. The truth is that perception is reality, and the early bird often gets the short shrift. The end of the day is usually when deadlines are due and last-minute projects are born, so those who are onsite and available when these things pop up are the ones who get noticed and rewarded. Fair? No. But that is the reality of the perception. Those who work later in the day get noticed and respected more than those who are all alone in the office at the crack of dawn.

9. **Promote your progress.**

   It is important that you keep your Workaholic Boss apprised of your accomplishments and progress. Because Workaholic Bosses are so hyper-focused on work, make sure they know that you are as well. Don't just assume that he knows the level of your productivity. Make your results obvious and provide progress reports on your projects. A weekly summary will not only help your boss appreciate your efforts, but it also provides an opportunity for your boss to adjust your priorities and confirm deadlines.

10. **Seek their advice and guidance.**

    Because Workaholics are generally passionate about work and have scads of experience under their belt, they can often make great mentors and teachers. Tap into their wisdom and experience. Chances are if they love to work, they will also love to *talk* about work.

11. **Know when to sacrifice.**

    Even if you are super productive every day, there will be times when you will need to sacrifice for the cause. Being willing to put in the extra hours when needed will show your boss that you are a dedicated team player. Danny is a self-described Workaholic Boss: "I try really hard not to impose my work habits on my team, but the reality is that sometimes projects and deadlines come up that require a few late nights and weekends. While I don't expect my staff to make a habit of working these kind of hours, I do expect them to pitch in when the circumstances call for it. Those who aren't willing to go the extra mile now and then don't fare well with me. I know that sounds harsh, but we work in a very competitive environment, and sometimes that means we all have to sacrifice to be successful."

12. **Decide what you really want and act accordingly.**

   The bottom line is that if you want work-life balance or if you are a live-to-work person then don't expect to succeed in an organization, profession, or industry where workaholism is the path to success. Choose a profession, organization, or industry that better suits your life plan. If, however, you want to succeed in one of these industries, climb the corporate ladder, or accelerate your career, then chances are you are going to having to outwork, outperform, and outlast your peers in both the reality and perception of productively, results, and commitment. I don't know too many highly successful entrepreneurs, CEOs, tech magnates, investment bankers, or law partners that got where they are by working 9 to 5. That is just the reality.

13. **Say yes to the dress.**

   All the consternation and teeth-gnashing about work-life balance has given Workaholics a bad name. If you love what you do, if you are passionate about your work and your work life, if you are gaining the skills and experience because you need (or want) to get promoted or accelerate your career, then go for it. This can be especially favorable to younger employees who are just starting out and don't yet have as many home and family responsibilities. Don't let others make you feel bad for wanting what you want or enjoying your compulsion to work. Just remember that when *you* are the boss, you must try very hard not to impose your workaholic ways onto others.

14. **Know the bottom line.**

   While your Workaholic Boss may not expect you to put in the extra hours, trust me, they will notice when you do and will always appreciate (and reward) those who do over those who don't. It's your choice.

Real-Life Story

After carefully weighing the pros and cons of her Workaholic Boss, Josephine decided to try to make it work. "Adapting to Heidi's style has been a career changer for me. And honestly,

(continued)

(continued)

I didn't have to sacrifice as much as I thought I would. I started staying late once or twice a week, and it really worked to my advantage. Because Heidi always stayed late, this gave me the opportunity to get one-on-one face time with her. That really changed the dynamic. Heidi quickly saw and felt my dedication. I know it's not 'right,' but I don't mind checking my work phone in the evening and responding to her with a brief 'Got it' or 'I'm on it.' It only takes a few minutes every evening. By showing her that I am willing to check in and put in extra effort, I've found that when I do say that I don't have enough time or bandwidth, she takes it to heart since she knows that I'm dedicated to the work. I also try to stay one step ahead. I make it a point to keep her informed on what I'm working on and what I will have done by the end of the week. For me, it's been worth it. She thinks I am the bee's knees and has championed me throughout the organization. It's opened a lot of doors. Best career move I ever made, and it only took six months of sacrifice."

Strategy Recap

- Weigh the pros and cons: A Workaholic Boss can help boost your career but often at the cost of increased stress and anxiety.
- Know before you go: Do your homework on your boss, the organization, and the industry so you know what the work expectations are.
- Figure out if your Workaholic Boss wants to see hours logged or work accomplished, then adjust accordingly. Give him what he wants.
- If your Workaholic Boss is impressed by results, put your productivity into overdrive.
- Align your boundaries with your boss's expectations.
- Don't assume. Your boss may be firing off e-mails at 8 p.m. just to get something off her plate; she may not need or want a response.
- Promote your progress by keeping your boss apprised of your accomplishments.
- Be prepared to make the sacrifice if that's what it takes (and is what you want).
- There is no shame in being a workaholic yourself; just try not to impose that ethos on others.

18

The Incompetent

"Never ascribe to malice that which is adequately explained by incompetence."
—Napoleon Bonaparte

Real-Life Story

Casey realized that she was part of the problem.

Casey, a young architectural designer, works for a partner at medium-sized design firm. She loves her job, her projects, and her clients. Her boss, Susan, not so much. Susan had owned her own, much smaller firm, and was recruited to join forces with Casey's firm as a full partner. The problem is that Susan turned out to be a disaster – she wasn't delivering; in fact, she was failing. And Casey was sick and tired of constantly saving Susan from her own incompetence. Casey went to work every day feeling angry, resentful, and even competitive with her boss. After spending a few minutes with Casey, we realized that her anger and resentment had blinded her from seeing the potential opportunities, options, and strategies before her. In fact, her attitude was making things worse for her.

(continued)

(*continued*)

Casey acknowledged that Susan's incompetence was causing tension among the other partners, and Casey accepted that the organization was not going to take corrective action anytime soon. Bringing Susan on board was an expensive (and very public) endeavor. Removing her so soon after her arrival would require a level of effort, legal fees, and emotionality that the other partners were not prepared to take on. Susan wasn't going anywhere soon. It was up to Casey to either make it work or to leave.

Casey (with a little prompting from us) decided to drop her resentment and try a little empathy. She put herself in Susan's shoes. She imagined what it must be like to have sold her own firm to join another and then struggle to get footing. Casey tried to imagine what it must be like to know you are failing, to feel your new partners' disappointment, and to know your key employee resents you. "Wow," Casey said, "now I actually feel kind of bad for her. That would suck. If it were me, I'd be really questioning my self-worth and competency. And I would hate having an employee like me who made it worse."

Once Casey dropped her anger and resentment, she was able to see the opportunity that the incompetent Susan presented her. If she could help make Susan successful, then the other partners would notice. She had an opportunity to protect their investment, save them from a difficult situation, and present herself as a problem solver and a leader. She decided to take on the challenge. In a matter of months, Casey had forged a new relationship with Susan. Instead of being her antagonist, she became her ally. She helped Susan learn the new organization and readily offered her technical skills to bolster where Susan was weak. While Susan is still not an ideal boss, Casey found a way to make lemonade out of her lemon boss. The other partners did indeed notice. Casey is now on partnership track herself. And it all started with a simple shifting of perspective.

Working for an Incompetent Boss can be nothing short of infuriating. Incompetent Bosses devastate morale, demolish productivity, and destroy motivation. Yet they exist everywhere. Organizations are notorious for promoting people for all the wrong reasons. As discussed earlier, organizations love to promote people for technical skills instead of managerial skills. This often creates problems when the technical expert turns out to be a totally incompetent manager. A manager's job requires a different skill set than that of a technical contributor. A manager's job is to manage the people, process, and resources. The other challenge of hiring competent managers is that, quite frankly, mistakes can be made. Incompetents slip through the cracks. And once they do, organizations are often reluctant to remove them for a host of reasons, including:

- Time and expense of finding them.
- Time and expense of replacing them.
- Reluctance to admit they made a mistake.
- Fear of losing the technical talent of the Incompetent.
- Political connections – the Incompetent may be strongly allied with the powers that be. Or even worse – they may be related!
- They don't know because the Incompetent does a great job of managing up to their own boss.

Signs of the Incompetent

The signs and complaints of working for the Incompetent Boss are myriad. If you've found yourself seeing or complaining about the following, then you may be working for an Incompetent.

Avoids decisions
Your boss can't make a decision to save his life. He waffles, waffles, waffles, and just when you think he can't possibly delay the decision any longer, he digs deep down and waffles some more.

Prefers inaction
Incompetents often have a proclivity for inaction; after all, if you don't do anything, you won't make any mistakes or look bad.

Makes bad choices

Your boss has an uncanny ability to choose the wrong path every time. It's as if she literally isn't connected to reality or doesn't understand your profession at all. This makes you wonder if no decision is better than her bad choices.

Passes the work

Incompetents are great at passing their work – all their work – on to their staff members. If you find you are consistently covering for your boss's ineptitude, you may be working for an Incompetent.

Hires the wrong people

Competent managers hire competent people. Incompetent managers hire incompetent people. It's a vicious circle.

Misses deadline

Does your boss regularly ignore or miss deadlines? Or fail to make or enforce them? Competent people focus on and get results. Incompetents don't.

Loves consultants but never heeds their advice

This is very common – incompetent managers love to look like they are actively engaged in progress, improvements, or innovation. They hire consultants and then do nothing with the advice. The reports just gather dust on their shelves.

Focuses on the wrong things

Does your boss love to focus on things that don't really matter? Perhaps he is more interested in the cover sheet of your report than the content. Or maybe he loves to discuss the process but not the product. Or maybe he is more concerned with the time sheets of his employees than with their actual work results.

Keeps you in the dark

The Incompetent Boss is often an equally incompetent communicator. Incompetents often fail to keep their staff informed on both important and routine matters. Whether they do it intentionally (information is power) or unintentionally (they just don't know why you need to know), the result is the same: You feel like you are groping in the darkness.

Fails upward

Your inept boss somehow managers to keep her job or even get promoted despite her incompetence.

Discover the Drivers: Understanding the Incompetent Boss

Incompetent Bosses exist for a host of reasons. One on end of the spectrum, Incompetents are good people who just lack the skills needed for success. On the other end of the spectrum are the Frauds, Incompetents who manage to talk their way into (and keep themselves in) positions for which they are in no way qualified. Either way, the drivers of this behavior usually stem from some sort of deficiency:

Lack of confidence

Sometimes Incompetents simply lack a basic sense of self-assuredness. Similar to the Pushover, they may lack confidence in their ability to make decisions, achieve results, and take risks. They lack the courage to stand up for themselves (and their employees). For some reason, either by nature or nurture, they lack the self-assurance needed to manage effectively.

Fear of failure

Fear of failure can be paralyzing. People who are terrified to make mistakes, fail, or look bad are prone to the path of least resistance, which means inactivity. For the Fraud, this fear of failure turns into a fear of being found out. Both fears are extremely damaging to the organization.

Lack of experience

Achieving competence – in anything – requires experience, exposure, and practice. Achieving competence also requires an opportunity and willingness to learn. Best-case scenario with this type of boss is that he or she is only temporarily incompetent. Take Ben's situation. Ben, a participant in one of our workshops, owned up to being an Incompetent: "I was definitely the Incompetent when I first took this manager's job. I had no idea what I was doing, so I did nothing. I needed to learn the job, learn the team, and learn the organization. It took me six months before I felt I had enough experience to actually start to manage. I know my team thought I was the biggest Incompetent ever! Luckily, I got myself together and we now have a very successful team."

Lack of people skills

Competent managers have to be able to manage people. This requires emotional intelligence, people skills, and communication skills. For some people, these soft skills do not come naturally. For others, they simply don't believe in them and don't believe they need them. Tragic but true.

Lack of technical expertise

Some incompetents have great people skills (think Michael Scott from *The Office*) but sorely lack the technical skills of management or technical skills of the profession. Without a technical understanding of the work being done, this type of Incompetent is incapable of providing useful guidance or sound advice.

Proven Strategies to Manage Up the Incompetent

1. **Diagnose the disorder.**

   Is your boss an Incompetent or a Fraud? Remember, Incompetents are often good people who just lack the skills or sensibilities needed for success. Frauds talk their way into positions for which they are not qualified. Frauds are basically con artists who succeed through the gift of gab, on the backs of other people, and are usually great at managing up themselves. Try to figure out which one you are working for as it will help you decide how you want to manage up (or not).

2. **Check yourself.**

   Is your boss really incompetent? Or does she have a different way of doing things than you would? Before labeling your boss an Incompetent, take a good look to make sure your judgment is sound and not coming from jealousy, spite, or ignorance.

3. **Pinpoint the problems.**

   Try to figure out exactly where and how the incompetence is causing problems. Does your team need more expert guidance? More information? Does your boss make rash decisions or no decisions? While you can't fix the entire problem of incompetence, if you can pinpoint and prioritize the problems, then you and your teammates can create specific strategies to address the deficiency. If your boss doesn't understand the context of decisions then perhaps you can create a one-page summary for him. If your boss neglects to make timely decisions, maybe you can request the authority to make them for him, or provide the rationale he needs.

4. **Try a little empathy.**

   Empathy goes a long way in dealing with Incompetents who are afraid of failure or lacking in experience. Put yourself in their shoes. What pressure are they under? What help do they need? How would you feel if you were elevated into a position that you weren't qualified for? How would you want your team to treat you? Unless you determine that your Incompetent Boss is a Fraud or a bad person, start out on the side of empathy and compassion.

5. **Look for the good bits.**

   Incompetents are often good at *something*. They got the job somehow. Find out what they *do* know, and learn from them. Do they have amazing technical skills? The gift of gab? A great network? Political connections? Whatever it is see if you can find it and learn from it or use it to your team's advantage. Going back to the example of Michael Scott, he was a notoriously awful manager, but it was revealed at some point in the series that he was actually an amazing salesperson. Find the good bits.

6. **Show them the way.**

   If you suspect that your Incompetent just lacks the experience or confidence, then show her the way. Instead of approaching your boss with disdain and derision, approach with compassion. Use your interactions to help teach your boss what she needs to know. Don't be snarky; be kind. Avoid being judgmental. I know it's frustrating to have to do this, but if Incompetents need to learn, they need to learn. You can either teach them or stew and suffer their incompetence. Try to be proactive.

7. **Step up. Compensate and cover.**

   Believe it or not, an Incompetent Boss may be a blessing in disguise. Look for opportunities to shine and advance your career by doing great work and becoming your boss's biggest asset. Find opportunities to compensate for your boss's weakness. Offer to cover for her when she is out. Offer to take on more responsibility (with more authority when possible) and projects. Fill in where your boss is weak. Encourage your team to do the same. Try not to worry if your boss gets the credit for your successful projects; success eventually gets noticed, and in organizations that usually means the team and/or department gets noticed too. Make your boss and your team look good and you will look good as well. Plus, people aren't stupid.

Your peers know, and they are the ones who often matter the most when it comes time to leave.

8. **Get a mentor.**

An Incompetent Boss isn't going to bring much to the table in terms of professional growth and development, so you must look outside this relationship for mentoring.

9. **Expose with extreme caution.**

Exposing Incompetents or unmasking the Fraud is an extremely delicate (and dangerous) maneuver. Proceed cautiously. Remember, your boss's boss hired her, so he is going to be reluctant to hear he made a mistake. HR invested in her, so they, too, are going to be reluctant to remove her. If she is protected politically or is related to the owner (the boss's daughter!) then exposing her incompetence may do more to jeopardize your career than hers. If you decide to expose, it has to be about more than your discomfort and annoyance; you must be able to show the dangerous effects of the ineptness. And you need to report it to the right people.

Real-Life Story

Mary learned the dangers of exposing a Fraud early in her career. Okay – that's me! Yes, I learned this lesson many years back when I was the public relations and events director for a children's non-profit organization. We were selected to partner with a super cool regional circus out of New York whose business model included an annual partnership with a charity outside of New York. The circus would carefully select the charity and then would partner with it to host a two-week engagement. Proceeds from the engagement would be split between the two organizations. It was a terrific opportunity for the selected non-profit to dramatically increase its public exposure and to raise a great deal of money. The charity was responsible for securing space, media, advertising, and ticket sales. It required a considerable investment of money and resources on both sides. We had to prove our ability to be a good partner. The selection process was rigorous and competitive. And we were chosen.

Although I was involved during the selection process, once we were chosen, my boss decided that I didn't have the experience to lead the project, so she hired Ann-Marie, a project manager from outside to run the project. I'd be lying if I didn't admit that I was a little disappointed. But it was a big and exciting project and I knew I was still going to be deeply involved – and really, it was a circus! How cool was that? The circus was a well-run enterprise. They were professional and savvy. They were cool. I was thrilled. And then I got to know Ann-Marie. It was probably our third conversation when my bulls**t meter started going off. Something wasn't quite right. She seemed all talk and no action. Disorganized. Focused on the wrong things. The ramp-up time was seven months and the circus gave us a complete blueprint for success; we just had to execute it. The first task, of course, was securing a location. But Ann-Marie was focused on graphics for our mailers, something that we didn't need for months. Weeks went by, nothing. In the meantime, I was working with my support counterpart at the circus providing information, building relationships, etc.

It was not long before it became evident (to me at least) that Ann-Marie was flailing. We had no site secured, no permits, no advertising plan – nothing on her list was getting done. I knew my boss well enough to know that I couldn't express my concerns to her. Her ego wouldn't accept that she had made a mistake, and she would dismiss my concerns as hard feelings that I didn't get to lead the project. The circus was getting nervous. After two months of inaction and no secured site, the circus leadership came to town. They had created a list of possible locations (which was supposed to be our job) and requested that Ann-Marie drive around the area with them to scout. Ann-Marie decided that driving around all day was a subordinate's job so sent me in her stead.

Long story short: I ratted her out. When they asked me what the real deal was, I told them. I exposed her. And not because I didn't like Ann-Marie – I actually did. I exposed her because of the enormous financial risk that failure presented to

(continued)

(continued)

both organizations. I loved my organization. I loved our mission. I also deeply respected the circus people. They had trusted us as partners and we were letting them down. I knew I could be fired but I couldn't just sit back and watch the train wreck.

Ann-Marie was dismissed within 48 hours, which I discovered when my boss called me into her office and told me that I was to take over the project. She suddenly expressed a great deal of confidence in me. While I'll never know what happened between my boss and the circus leaders, I do know that I never suffered any repercussions. They were honorable people and somehow protected me from my boss's wrath.

Strategy Recap

- Determine which type of boss you have – an Incompetent or a Fraud.
- Check your own ego – is your boss Incompetent or are you just jealous?
- Pinpoint where exactly the incompetence is.
- Try a little tenderness – empathy goes a long way toward understanding an Incompetent.
- Try to find something good about the Incompetent.
- If your Incompetent needs to learn, be the one to teach.
- Step up, compensate, deliver, and make your Incompetent look good. You will get noticed.
- Don't rely on your Incompetent to be your mentor. Find someone else.
- Exposing your Incompetent can be dangerous, so proceed with caution.

19

The Nitpickers and Seagulls

"Why should we look to the past in order to prepare for the future? Because there is nowhere else to look."

—James Burke

While Nitpickers and Seagulls may not rise to the level of the truly difficult boss from hell, their tendencies to dive in or nitpick can be extremely annoying. Left unchecked or unmanaged, nitpicking and swooping behaviors can demotivate and annoy even the most engaged worker.

The Nitpicker

Nitpickers love to, well, nitpick. Nothing is ever perfect enough. They dive into the most miniscule details. Instead of praising (or even acknowledging) the good parts of your work, they focus on the one error they find. Their attention to detail feels pathological and their red pen is their best friend. They nitpick your choices – "Make that graph blue, not red," "Use the word 'cooperate,' not 'collaborate,'" etc. They deep dive into details that seem to suggest they have too much time on their hands.

161

Real-Life Story

Jennifer was asked to work on a project for her boss's boss. It was an internal research project that her boss's boss needed for background information. She had clear guidance from the boss's boss, yet her boss kept diving and nitpicking, even after the boss's boss had approved the format. "It was always just little things, like if I made a spreadsheet, he would go through each column and ask for changes to the text size or font or shade of the color. I would think, let me finish the data gathering and then we can work out the details! It felt like a huge waste of time to me."

Discover the Drivers: Understanding the Nitpicker

It's easy to label and dismiss Nitpickers as Micromanagers. And that would be a mistake. While many Micromanagers do tend to be Nitpickers, not all Nitpickers are Micromanagers. This is an important distinction. You can have a boss who allows you lots of freedom to work on your project, then nitpicks it at the end. Micromanagers are about control; Nitpickers are about perfection, standards, and preferences.

In order to understand what drives the Nitpicker, here is what a few self-described Nitpickers say:

- *I just want it to be perfect. At the end of the day, my name is associated with this product so I need it to be accurate and polished. I have high standards and expect the same from my team.*
- *I look for consistency in my staff's work. I'm not so much bothered by their choices as long as they are consistent. For example, if you are going to use the Oxford comma, then use the Oxford comma throughout. Inconsistency drives me crazy. To me, it is sloppy.*
- *I have a certain graphic sensibility that I want my team to follow. The look of our products is important to me. I know I drive my team crazy, but I want our products to have a consistent visual image. I want things to look good and match our brand.*

Proven Strategies to Manage Up the Nitpicker

1. **Check yourself first.**

   Are you the only one being nitpicked? Or does she nitpick every-one? If you are the only one, then you need to take a rigorous review of your work. If you are mistake prone, clean it up. Triple proof your work. Take responsibility to clean up your act.

2. **Learn what they like.**

   This is key. In order to please Nitpickers, you need to learn what pleases them. Pay attention to what they nitpick over. Learn their style and preferences. Don't guess. Ask. Before you take on a project ask questions about the final result. What is important to them? What preferences do they have? What are their font preferences? Do they have particular graphics in mind? When you get back a marked-up product, meet with the Nitpicker. Ask why he prefers the Oxford comma or that particular font, word, graphic, etc. Don't be snarky, be curious. If you really feel that the Oxford comma isn't appropriate for this report, listen to your boss's reasons first, then tactfully present a different view.

3. **Adopt their standards.**

   Nitpickers have high standards. Once you discover their stan-dards and preferences, then adopt them. If your Nitpicker wants error-free work, then deliver error-free work. It's as simple as that.

4. **Resist the urge to resist.**

   Resisting a Nitpicker's preference is silly and futile. Resisting just wastes time and emotional energy. If your Nitpicker wants things a certain way, then make it so. Instead of grousing about how you hate the Oxford comma, just use it. If your boss likes blue head-ings, then big deal, use blue. If your boss changes a word on a document three times that results in your original word being used, don't sweat it. Don't expend a bunch of emotional energy around minutiae. Make the changes and move on.

Real-Life Story

Mary was driving Laura crazy. Mary – who is normally a ter-rific boss – had this annoying habit of going into Laura's slide

(continued)

(*continued*)

decks and changing the graphics. "I spent a lot of time choosing graphics, and then Mary would just change them. It drove me crazy. I liked my graphic choices! Then one day, I decided to ask her why she did it. She explained to me her rationale on choosing graphics, and it suddenly made sense. While I don't necessarily agree with all of her choices, at least now I understand what she likes and I do my best to choose ones that I think she will approve. I don't know why I didn't ask her sooner. I would have saved myself a lot of teeth gnashing."

The Seagull Boss: Poopers and Poachers

Seagulls swoop, and there are actually two types of Seagulls: poopers and poachers. The pooper Seagulls are those who swoop in at the last minute (or at the first sign of trouble), poop on everything, and then swoop out. They make lots of noise, create a big mess, and leave it to the team to clean up. The pooper Seagull is particularly annoying because he hasn't been involved in the details of the project and his poop isn't helpful, just stressful.

The second type of Seagull, the poacher, is the boss who assigns you a project and then, when you are almost done, swoops in and poaches it for herself. This leaves you feeling annoyed, dispirited, and often unappreciated. You also may feel like you've just wasted hours and weeks of your time. Poachers often seem to have an uncanny ability to do this on projects that you actually enjoy.

Real-Life Story

Tina was the program director for a marketing association. She loved her job, but her boss was driving her crazy. "I'll be in the home stretch of a really cool project, then my boss will swoop in and take the project for himself. It's very annoying. I'm happy to collaborate on the project, it's just frustrating that he waits until I am almost done to take it for himself. It feels like I've just wasted weeks of work."

Discover the Drivers: Understanding the Seagull

Understanding the Seagull Boss is difficult since the behavior could stem from several intrapersonal dynamics and/or environmental circumstances.

Lack of emotional intelligence
Seagulls who swoop and poop are often lacking in emotional intelligence, impulse control, and people skills. They panic, then poop.

Lack of project awareness
Some Seagulls swoop because they lack knowledge about the project or work. Perhaps they haven't been paying attention or haven't been provided proper project updates. They may suddenly come to realize the importance of a project or learn about a project snag. Then they swoop in to save the day.

Lack of trust
At the end of the day, many Seagulls may not trust that you or the team will execute properly. Try as they might, they lose trust, then they panic, and the swooping commences.

External events
A swoop may sometimes be the result of external circumstances. Maybe *they* got swooped. Maybe your project suddenly became a trophy project. Maybe your project just became an organizational priority. Suddenly, your project is their priority or maybe even their thorn, so they swoop.

Proven Strategies to Manage Up the Seagull

1. **Who's swooping whom?**
   As with most difficult boss behaviors, look around to see if you are the only one being swooped. If so, there may be something that you are doing or not doing that is causing your boss to swoop you. It may be the nature of your work – perhaps you work on cool stuff that your Seagull wants to take back. Or maybe it's the quality of your work, in the case of the pooper Seagull. The former is about inclusion, the latter about trust.

2. **Anticipate the swoop.**

   If you have a Seagull Boss, don't let the swoop surprise you. If your boss is a poacher, then pay attention to the types of projects she likes to poach. There is usually a pattern. Does she poach projects that are highly visible? Does she tend to poach when projects are delayed? Does she poach after some internal or external event, such as a meeting with her boss or the board of directors? Pay attention to the environment as well. Some poachers poach when the work product suddenly gains traction, attention, or industry relevance. The more you can anticipate the swoop, the less jarring it will be when it happens.

3. **The same goes for the Poopers.**

   Try to identify what drives the swoop. If you can pinpoint the pattern, you may be able to prevent the poop, or at least minimize it. Does your Seagull start to panic at deadline time? Is he operating from a lack of information? Is *she* reporting to a Seagull? Does your boss poop on you after his boss poops on him? Forewarned is forearmed.

4. **Communication is king.**

   Whether your Seagull is a pooper or poacher, keeping her in the loop is essential. Don't be fooled by her seeming disinterest. If she has a habit of swooping, then you must make a habit of looping. At the start of the project, find out what kind of involvement your boss wants or needs. Provide regular updates on project status. Schedule project review meetings. Keep your boss informed of potential delays, snags, or problems. If you suspect that the project is something swoop-able, then go to your boss first.

Real-Life Story

Danny worked for a small consulting company that specialized in training and facilitation. He learned how to anticipate and manage his Seagull Bosses by being proactive in his communication. "The partners I worked for had an annoying habit of swooping in and taking over my projects. At first, I was totally annoyed. I couldn't understand why they hired me if they were going to just take over my projects. Then, I started noticing a pattern, they would poach projects that were new, like if I was designing a new class or training. It's as if they suddenly realized that this program was happening and they wanted to be a part of it. Once I figured out their pattern, I started asking for their involvement at the beginning. I made it a point to provide regular updates and sought their feedback frequently on the new projects. For the most part, it's worked great. While they still swoop now and then, it's not nearly as bad as it was."

5. **Keep calm and carry on.**

   While the Seagull Boss who poaches is annoying and dispiriting, it's not necessarily the end of the world. Losing an occasional cool project is a bummer, but try to look forward and onward to the next project. If, however, your poacher poaches all the cool projects, then it may be time to look elsewhere for work. Take a calm and honest review of the poached projects. If you are losing more than you are gaining, then wave goodbye to the Seagull. Tina, discussed earlier, did in fact, decide that the poaching was a big enough problem for her to leave: "*Honestly, I had to leave. The whole reason I took this job was because of the types of projects that my boss kept poaching. At the end of the day, I wasn't learning or growing so I decided to pack it up and take my skills elsewhere.*"

   Keeping calm is essential if your Seagull Boss is a pooper. Try not to take your boss's rants personally. I know it is easier said than done, but try to imagine that you are wearing a poop-proof anorak. Let the ranter rant, then carry on. And of course, always weigh the pros and cons. While I can never justify treating people poorly – especially coming from managers – only you can judge the tipping point between the occasional annoying emotional outburst and repeated grievous emotional abuse.

Real-Life Story

Chris knew his boss was a seagull – the pooping kind. "Everyone knew that our boss, Oskar, was a Seagull. It happened toward the end of every quarter. As the production numbers started to get real for the quarter, Oskar would suddenly get very focused and more than a little vexed. He'd call us into his office, squawk around, flap his wings, spew some criticism, and then kick us out of his office. Honestly, we got so used to it, that we all actually found it kind of funny. Besides his occasional swoops, he was a decent boss and the job was good. So, we just let his storms pass and then carried on."

Strategy Recap

Nitpickers

- Learn what they like.
- Ask about their preferences, standards, and expectations.
- Adopt their high standards.
- Learn to accept that is who they are.

Seagulls

- Pay attention to when, where, and how your Seagull poops.
- Anticipate and plan for the swoop.
- Keep your Seagull Boss in the loop.
- Keep calm and carry on.

20

The Truly Terrible – Psycho Crazy Bully Tyrannical Screaming Egomaniacs

"He who knows when he can fight and when he cannot, will be victorious."
—Sun Tzu, *The Art of War*

Real-Life Story

Several years ago, I was at the dentist for my semi-annual cleaning and checkup. I'd only had this dentist for a about a year or so, as Dr. X had bought the practice from my former dentist. Dr. X was okay. He was a bit of an "overseller" but hey, I only had to see him twice a year. I did, however, adore my hygienist, Ella. She was from Serbia and was a tough cookie. She was funny and honest. When Dr. X would try to upsell me on things I didn't need, Ella would shoot me a quick wink, which meant "Ignore him." So, on this day, Ella had finished my cleaning and we were chit-chatting while I waited for Dr. X to come in and do the dental exam. After five minutes or so, I asked if he was coming

(continued)

(*continued*)

in soon (Ella knows that I am always in a hurry). "Oh, he should be in any minute," Ella assured me. Just then, I started hearing a heated conversation in the room next door. Voices got louder, and one voice got extremely loud.

Naturally, at first, I was fascinated – I love to eavesdrop on a good argument – then the loud voices turned to screaming, and then the screaming got really bad; it started sounding abusive. Someone was berating somebody else very badly. It went from interesting to horrifying really fast. Ella got very quiet. Then suddenly it struck me – the screaming bully was my dentist! "Ella! Is that Dr. X doing the screaming?" She very quietly said yes. Dr. X was yelling at the office manager, whose office was next to my exam room. I've honestly never heard anything like the tirade he unleashed on that poor woman. I sat there for 20 minutes listening to him berate and bully this employee. I asked Ella if this behavior was typical, and, again, she said yes. I told Ella that I was leaving and was never coming back. I told her she needed to find another job. She just smiled and shrugged her shoulders and said, "I need this job." Ella had become accustomed to the abuse. I left.

A few years after this incident, my husband and I read an article in the *Washington Post* about a dentist who was arrested (and later convicted) of sexually abusing patients while they were under sedation. Guess who that dentist was? You guessed it: Dr. X.

The Truly Terrible are everywhere. These are the bosses who are not just difficult to deal with, but are truly psycho, crazy, bullying, tyrannical, screaming egomaniacs. These are the bosses who use dominance, power, and control to lead. These are the bosses who are emotional (and sometimes physical) abusers. These are the bosses who are unyielding control freaks, blamers, manipulators, and tyrants. They thrive on intimidating, bullying, humiliating, and browbeating their staff. They are extreme Narcissists who refuse to take responsibility for their actions. They are unstable, and they lie, cheat, and steal their way to the top. They are Truly Terrible, and they are everywhere.

Truly Terrible Bosses are thriving in America and apparently elsewhere. A recent study showed that this type of self-focused boss is not only prevalent but may also be on the rise in the United States and other Western countries. Study after study confirms that the Truly Terrible are everywhere. Studies show that over 40 percent of workers have suffered from verbal, emotional, or even physical abuse from a supervisor at some point in their career. Research also clearly demonstrates the damaging impact that these bosses have on organizational morale, culture, climate, employee retention, engagement, and even productivity. One often-reported study says that these bosses cost the economy well over $350 billion each year from lost productivity. Sadly, their organizations do nothing about it. Research shows that working for a psycho, crazy, bully, tyrannical, screaming, egomaniac boss literally damages the employee's health. One study in Sweden showed that employees who work for the Truly Terrible were 60 percent more likely to suffer a heart attack, stroke, or other life-threatening cardiac condition. Other studies in American workplaces show that people who are stuck working for the Truly Terrible are more susceptible to chronic stress, depression, and anxiety, which increases the risk of a lowered immune system, colds, strokes, and even heart attacks. Truly Terrible Bosses make employees physically and emotional sick, and these conditions cost the organization money in health costs and sick days. Yet organizations do nothing.

The Truly Terrible Boss directly affects an organization's bottom line. Employees who are constantly bullied and berated lose motivation, get sick, and are too stressed to perform at high levels. These Truly Terrible cost their employers real bottom-line money due to the cost of employee turnover, lowered productivity, and legal fees. One organization that did the math on one of their Truly Terrible supervisors discovered that this one boss cost them over *$160,000 in one year* due to his bad behavior.

Signs of the Truly Terrible

The difference between the annoying or difficult boss and the Truly Terrible is a matter of frequency and potency. It is important to identify how *often* your boss exhibits the behavior and how *forceful* that behavior is. For example, a boss who occasionally throws a temper tantrum, says mean things, and threatens to fire you is terrible, but a boss who frequently and regularly rages at you, demeans, humiliates, and punishes you is Truly Terrible. Take a look at the list below. Rate your boss on a scale of 1 (meaning rarely) to 5 (meaning daily) and the velocity of the behavior (from 1 mild to 5 severe). Think about the frequency and severity.

Does your boss:

1. Yell, scream, curse, or shout at you (or others)? How frequently? How badly?
2. Refuse to accept responsibility or blame? Blame you or others for his "errors"? How frequently? How badly?
3. Give you unreasonable job demands, deadlines, or goals? How frequently? How badly?
4. Threaten you with pay cuts or being fired? How frequently? How badly?
5. Malign your competency, insult you, and/or criticize your abilities? Does this happen in front of others? How frequently? How badly?
6. Fly into temper tantrums or rages? How frequently? How badly?
7. Cross ethical lines? How frequently? How badly?
8. Exclude you from team meetings and communication channels, or give you the silent treatment? How frequently? How badly?
9. Change the rules on you or have different rules for different people? How frequently? How badly?
10. Deny, discount, ignore, or minimize your accomplishments? Take credit for your results? How frequently? How badly?
11. Exploit and manipulate you or others? How frequently? How badly?
12. Pit team members against each other? Create divisions between those in favor and those out of favor? How frequently? How badly?
13. Demonstrate a significant lack of empathy, sympathy, or insensitivity to others? How frequently? How badly?
14. Act with an air of superiority, pomposity, and/or condescension? How frequently? How badly?
15. Display insincerity, duplicity, or two-facedness? How frequently? How badly?

16. Engage in name-calling or other acts that embarrass or humiliate their targets? How frequently? How badly?
17. Exhibit extreme impatience, lack of focus, or impulse control? How frequently? How badly?
18. Need to always be right? Refuse to listen to the ideas of others? How frequently? How badly?
19. Demand absolute loyalty but will throw you under the bus at the first opportunity? How frequently? How badly?
20. Crack under pressure? Freak out when the going gets tough? How frequently? How badly?

If your score for both velocity and frequency was under 80, you may be dealing with a difficult boss, but not necessarily a Truly Terrible. If your score is over 80, then be aware and start strategizing. A score that is over 160? Get out. *Now.*

Real-Life Story

Many, many years ago, when I was 28 years old, I worked for a screaming, rage-prone, two-faced, micromanaging elected official. He was a popular "man of the people" but a terrible manager. While I could have dealt with any one of those traits in isolation, the combination and potency of those behaviors was just too much. I had to make a choice: stay in survival mode and watch my career die a slow death, or I could leave. I left and started my own business. That was the last boss I ever had. When I told my Truly Terrible Boss that I was leaving to start a business, he was incredulous that anyone would leave his employ. He made a point of telling me (three times) that I would fail. Then he never spoke to me again.

Understanding the Truly Terrible

The Truly Terrible probably suffer from a combination of personality disorders, dysfunctions, and maladies. Perhaps they are clinically depressed, sociopathic, or psychopathic. Perhaps they are Narcissists to the nth degree. Perhaps they are power hungry. Or insecure. Or out of their comfort zone. Or under extreme personal and/or professional pressure. Or maybe their mother didn't love them. Or maybe they are just damaged individuals. Their behavior is so egregious, it can only be described as pathological. This is the one boss where, frankly, what drives them doesn't really matter because at the end of the day, they don't care about you. They only care about their agenda. They lack the desire and capacity for self-reflection. They will never change because they will never see the need for it. And why should they? If their organizations aren't holding them accountable, who will? If they are rewarded for their behavior, why should they change? And if your Truly Terrible Boss is the owner of the company, well then, good luck to you.

Bottom Line for the Truly Terrible

> **Bottom Line**
>
> You can't win with the Truly Terrible. They are too damaged, too dangerous, too self-absorbed.

If your boss is only a borderline Truly Terrible, then you might be able to survive and even thrive – for a while. If your answers to the above questions were a handful of 1s or 2s, then you might be able to make some lemonade out of your lemons. Maybe.

> **Real-Life Story**
>
> Phil made it work with his borderline Truly Terrible for nearly 17 years. Phil was the number two man at a small consumer marketing company. He described his boss, Kevin, the owner and CEO, as "a borderline tyrant who loved to play the martyr." Kevin was extremely condescending and passive-aggressive to the staff. He was impossible to please. Nobody could work hard enough to prove themselves to Kevin, because nobody could ever work as hard or care as much as Kevin. He demanded complete loyalty and expected his staff to work around the clock like he did. If you dared to take a vacation that lasted more

than two or three days, Kevin would give you the cold shoulder, take you off high-profile projects, and subject you to a barrage of passive-aggressive comments when you returned.

"I began working for Kevin when he first started the company. I think I was the third employee," Phil said. "I was able to build trust with him early on because for a long time it was him and me in the trenches together. As the business grew, so did his inability to develop positive leadership skills. The best way to sum it up is that, on the surface, he tried to behave like a good boss and did meet some of those expectations, but he clearly had an internal struggle that he couldn't reconcile. He's somebody who rationally tried to approach being a leader by imitating the positive attributes of a good leader, but from an emotional standpoint, he never succeeded. It was often painful to watch him attempt to connect on a human level with the team. When he was upset or you disagreed with him, he would try to adopt a happy and light tone, and that's when you would know that he wasn't being genuine. The tone always turned condescending and the pitch of his voice would get very aggressive. There were inferences and innuendos. It was very obvious. You didn't even have to read between the lines. You knew that he was upset, that he was not even willing to see another perspective. I think he was basically incapable of recognizing or valuing the staff's needs, perspectives, or worth. They only mattered to him as a means to an end. And they knew it."

Phil explained that he stayed for so long because of several reasons. One, he was learning a great deal from Kevin about running a business and about the marketing industry. Two, he felt a sense of duty to the staff to be a calming, kind presence between them and Kevin, a buffer role he took seriously. And last, he stayed because for a long time he was able to deal with Kevin through deflection and avoidance.

"I survived for a long time by grinning, bucking up, and avoiding. But then, in the last few years, I made some changes in how I approached my own personal life and I decided I was

(continued)

> *(continued)*
>
> not going to play the avoidance strategy. When there were things that were important to talk about – personally and professionally – I needed to have the courage to talk about them. So, I started having these honest dialogues with Kevin, and it didn't go well at all. I would approach those conversations very carefully because I knew what was at stake. Nevertheless, being honest with Kevin backfired completely. It was the nail in my coffin when it came to my future there."

When you find yourself working for someone who waved goodbye at the border and is now fully ensconced in the camp of the Truly Terrible, then you need to protect yourself until you can leave. The longer you stay, the more you are damaging your health and future prospects. Research shows that it takes up to 22 months to emotionally and psychologically recover from the trauma of a psycho, crazy, bully, tyrannical, screaming, egomaniac boss.

The only people who can win with this type of boss are those who support, adopt, and/or emulate the boss's behavior. If you are willing to become a henchman for your bully boss, go for it. If you are willing to be part of the problem, then do so knowing that you are a killer of souls and are damaging your bottom line.

Strategies That Probably Won't Work and Might Even Backfire

Because the Truly Terrible are so beyond the pale, conventional strategies may not work. In addition, institutional support for dealing with the Truly Terrible may be weak or ineffective. Good luck.

1. **HR might be helpless.**

   Going to HR may be an option. Unfortunately, it's not frequently a good one. This is in no way meant to malign the good people who work in HR. Most of them mean well and probably care deeply. The problem is that they usually don't have any power. Or they have the wrong kind of power. So much depends on the size of your company, the role and purview of HR, and the culture of your company. If your VP of HR sits on the executive team as an equal business and strategy partner with the other executives *and* the positive culture of your company is truly valued and tended to, then you might have a chance. But these types of HR departments are rare. In most organizations, HR is more about employee compensation, benefits, employment agreements, and keeping the organization out of legal hot water. HR managers who report to the CFO or other "technical" leader probably have no power. It may do more harm than good. Make yourself aware of your HR department's reputation in supporting employee complaints before you approach.

2. **Confrontation is chancy.**

   Confronting a bully head-on is extremely difficult. While you should always stand up for yourself and set boundaries, going toe-to-toe with the Truly Terrible is rarely productive. People who willingly (and gleefully) treat other people in an abusive fashion are not going to take this conversation well. Confronting them on their behavior may just give them more fodder. It's like poking the bear. If you do confront the bully, plan your conversation wisely. Frame your requests unemotionally. Research or seek help from experts on how to conduct this conversation.

3. **Your colleagues have no power.**

   If you are the sole target or part of a chosen target group, then asking colleagues to intervene on your behalf may prove fruitless. If your boss is really a Truly Terrible, then your favored friends could be putting themselves in the line of fire by coming to your defense. Even if they are willing to do it, the odds of their ending up in the same boat as you are high.

4. **Mediation? Maybe.**

   Mediation is another often-touted option. Again, this might work, and it might not. I've known very few people who found effective relief from a psycho, crazy, bully, tyrannical, screaming egomaniac with mediation. Mediation might work when your boss is simply annoying or bad, but mediation with the Truly Terrible? I don't think so. Mediation works when two parties can come together to openly discuss their differences and come to some mutually agreed-on resolution. The problem with this strategy is that most of the Truly Terrible are completely incapable of any self-reflection or willingness to accept responsibility for the impact of their behavior. This may make you an even larger target.

5. **Beware Your Boss's Boss.**

Going to your boss's boss is another risky strategy. Chances are your boss's boss hired your boss and therefore feels committed to him. The Truly Terrible are able to stay in organizations through high achievement, political prowess, and great managing-up skills. Chances are their boss is one of their biggest fans or afraid to address the issue. Either way, it doesn't bode well for you.

Real-Life Story

Angie worked for a Truly Terrible named Peter. "When the exploitation and verbal abuse became too much to handle, I tried talking to his boss. That was a big mistake," she said. "Peter's boss, Joanna, told Peter that I was complaining about him, and his behavior got even worse. Then I requested a mediation, something that our organization offers. Peter's boss refused. She said that she had bad experiences with these types of mediators in the past, so she didn't want anything to do with them. She thought it reflected poorly on her ability to manage. So now I was totally persona non grata. The thought of going above Joanna's head was more than I could handle. I was too demoralized to keep trying. I had to get out, so I quit."

---

6. **Blow the whistle? Take a deep breath first.**

I truly and deeply admire whistle-blowers. They are the true workplace warriors and champions of all that is good in the world of work (and politics and every other part of the human experience you can think of). I would hire a whistle-blower any day of the week. But sadly, I'm not a corporate titan. And I am probably in the minority. The truth is, while whistle-blowing is, hands down, the right thing to do, it can often spell disaster for the whistle-blower. That is, even if you have someone to blow the whistle to. Consider the fact that large businesses only employ about 38 percent of the private sector workforce while small businesses employ 53 percent of the workforce. To make matters more challenging, more than

95 percent of these small businesses have fewer than 10 employees. If you blow the whistle in your small business, who is going to care? If you blow the whistle in your large business, you may have a fighting chance. Know that you are going up against an army of lawyers and public relations warriors. Whistle-blowing is the right thing to do – just make sure you understand the game and arm yourself appropriately. In a perverse way, it may be easier to go up against a Fortune-500 company than Joe Shmo's Acme Air Conditioning and Shoe Repair. No offense to Joe Shmo.

Strategies That Might Work

No one can work for a psycho, crazy, bully, tyrannical, screaming, egomaniac boss long term and thrive. The following strategies are meant as temporary survival strategies. They are designed to give you time to look for a better (or just different) job.

1. **Adopt a survivor mentality.**
   As with any survival situation, it is important to externalize the situation. It is what it is. Instead of expending emotional energy on "why" or "why me," accept that it is happening and use your energy to devise and implement strategies to survive. This is a difficult situation. You need to maintain as much objectivity as possible in order to survive and escape. Commit your energy to survival and escape strategies.
2. **Distance yourself.**
   In order to survive, you have to create an emotional distance between yourself and the abusive boss. When she screams, let it just bounce off you. When she berates you, just roll your eyes (internally, of course). When she stomps around and intimidates, find humor in her performance. When she blames you for her mistakes, just smile knowingly. Tune out the drama, turn on the kindness. Tell yourself that her bullying has nothing to do with you, feel sorry for her because her behavior is ridiculous, and then give her a genuine smile and agree to attend to whatever "disaster" she's bemoaning. Remember, you can't manage another person's actions; you can only manage your own *reaction*. Giving yourself distance helps you choose your reaction.

3. **Protect your psyche.**

   This is probably the most important thing you can do. At the beginning of every day, imagine you are putting on a golden shield or force field around your soul. This golden shield needs to keep you from internalizing the behaviors and impact. Visualize your force field or shield blocking your boss's poison arrows. It sounds flaky, but it really works. Do what you can to prevent the internalization of their attacks. Protect your psyche.

4. **Maintain your professionalism.**

   Keep doing the job you were hired to do. Maintain high-quality work habits. Document your accomplishments. Track your results. Don't let the Truly Terrible throw you off your game. Continue to show up to work on time and complete your projects in a timely and professional manner. Keep a record of your assignments and your results. It's important that you don't provide any fodder for the Truly Terrible by turning in sloppy or late work. Maintain an outward image of high self-esteem, competency, and professionalism.

5. **Stay out of the line of fire.**

   Do what you can to remove yourself from as much contact as possible. Identify safe spots; sometimes the Truly Terrible are reluctant to show their colors in front of others. When in the midst of an outburst, do what you can to excuse yourself in a calm and rational manner. Try to lie low and fly under the radar as much as possible.

6. **Activate your support network.**

   Having a strong support network is critical when dealing with a survival situation. Make sure you have appropriate professional and personal support and contact. Inside the organization, keep connected to your coworkers. Volunteer to work on assignments outside your boss's domain. Build your network. Attend industry events. The more internal and external contacts you make and relationships you build, the easier it will be to find a new opportunity and execute your escape. In your personal life, seek the support of friends and confidants. Find other outlets – such as volunteering – where you can feel fulfilled and validated. Have outlets outside of work for socializing and reducing stress. Talk to a coach, therapist, or other trained professional. Surround yourself with friends and people who support you.

7. **Take care of yourself.**

The research is clear: Working for a Truly Terrible boss is bad for your physical and mental health. Cultivate coping strategies as best you can. Meditate, exercise, get sleep, and go visit your doctor. Your health and well-being are far more important than this job.

8. **Plan your exit.**

Again, working for the Truly Terrible is no way to endure the majority of your waking hours. You should start planning your exit as soon as possible. Get your résumé updated. Activate your network. Search out other opportunities both within and outside your organization. Please know that your exit may not be of your own volition. If you are the only or one of the only targets of your Truly Terrible Boss, you just might find yourself on the receiving end of a pink slip. I've talked to dozens of people who were special targets of their bully boss and eventually got the axe. Be prepared. Don't feel ashamed. This just may be your silver lining.

Real-Life Story

Ellen, who is now a highly successful marketing executive in the legal field, knew something was wrong almost immediately when she started to work for a small event-planning firm. "My boss just didn't like me," she said. "She was horrible to me starting on day one. She would berate me in front of others, blame me for everything, and demand my attention 24/7. She was unethical and expected me to follow in her footsteps. I used to sit in my car and cry every morning before I could enter the building. I had friends lined up for daily pep talks. I was so afraid of being jobless that I just thought if I tried harder, if I worked smarter, she would treat me differently. Nothing I tried worked. Then one day, she just fired me. I was devastated. I was embarrassed and ashamed.

(continued)

(continued)

In fact, in all these years, I've never admitted to anyone that I was fired from that job. It took me a while to lick my wounds, but I soon realized that being fired was the best thing that ever happened to me. It led me to my current position, working at a wonderful company that values and appreciates me. I just wish I could tell my younger self that getting fired isn't the end of the world!"

9. **Document everything.**

   It's important to keep a paper trail of your boss's abuse, in case you do decide to go to HR or seek legal recourse. When your boss demonstrates abusive behavior, take note of it and keep the records in a safe place, and preferably *not* on company equipment. Be sure to note the time and date as well as the names of any witnesses or other targets. Be sure to note incidents of abuse toward others too, as this may help illustrate a pattern of abuse. Keep copies of e-mails and other written correspondence that expose abusive conduct or communication.

10. **Make the business case.**

    If you choose to alert leadership about your Truly Terrible Boss, then do so by making a business case that this boss is too expensive to keep on board. Gather data on turnover costs, productivity costs, absenteeism costs, legal costs, etc. While some organizations care about employee self-esteem, *all* organizations care about the bottom line. There are several organizations, such as the Workplace Bullying Institute (workplacebullying.org) that can help you develop a business case.

11. **Seek expert support.**

    Dealing with a truly abusive boss is a very serious and potentially life-threatening situation. Do not hesitate to seek expert support and guidance. Consult with workplace bullying experts. Talk to an employment lawyer. Speak with professionals who specialize in these matters. Their guidance and support can help you explore your options and create a successful strategy.

Strategy Recap: These Probably Won't Work and Might Even Backfire

- HR may be helpful but only if your HR department has the right kind of power.
- If you do confront the bully, plan your conversation wisely and know that it will likely backfire.
- Don't draw your colleagues in or expect them to help you.
- Mediation probably won't work, but it might be worth a try.
- Your boss's boss might be her ally, so tread carefully if you are thinking of going over the Truly Terrible's head.
- Think long and hard about blowing the whistle.

Strategy Recap: These Might Work

- Adopt a survivor mentality.
- Distance yourself.
- Protect your psyche – don a golden shield.
- Maintain your professionalism and productivity.
- Stay out of the line of fire as much as you can.
- Activate your support network and take care of yourself.
- Document everything, just in case you go the legal or HR route.
- Plan your exit: Get your résumé and other docs in order.
- Getting fired may not be the worst thing to happen.

21

It's Okay to Quit

"If at first you don't succeed, try, try again. Then quit. There's no point in being a damn fool about it."

—W.C. Fields

Quitting is an act of courage. I don't take quitting lightly.

Quitting is not in my nature. In fact, for the first quarter of my life, quitting was a dirty word. It was abhorrent to me. It was shameful. Growing up, my family motto was "quitters never win." That motto was drilled into us kids by my (well-meaning) parents. Both parents grew up poor and built a successful life through grit, hard work, and persistence. So, for them, quitting was a weakness and should be avoided at all costs. As children and young adults, my siblings and I were stuck with any commitments we made. Hate the basketball team? Tough luck; you wanted to play, so now you have to see the season out. Hate guitar lessons (which I did)? Tough luck; you made a commitment to play. Hate honors algebra? Too bad. Do your best. Hate babysitting? Suck it up; you said you wanted to earn extra money. Hate working at the local pizza joint? Too bad; you took the job. And so on and so on.

I took this mantra into my adulthood and my professional life. Quitting was for losers. Quitting made you weak. Quitting was what quitters do, and quitters never win.

While sticking things out is a noble and often useful tenet, experience has taught me that quitting is also empowering. I have come to believe that quitting can be an act of creativity, growth, and empowerment. There are times where quitting is and should be the best course of action.

Should You Go or Should You Stay?

Quitting is a spectrum. If you quit at the slightest sign of difficulty or trouble, then you risk losing out on valuable lessons and experiences. You may fail to develop grit. Staying inside our comfort zone keeps us from learning and growing. On the other end of the spectrum, staying with someone or something that destroys your soul, makes you unhappy, or sucks your energy away from something useful in your life is nonsensical. Only you can decide what is best for you.

Signs It's Time to Quit

- You wake up miserable every day and dread going to work. On Sunday nights you feel as if you are heading to prison the next day.
- Your physical and emotional well-being are being damaged.
- You feel unsafe (physically or emotionally) at work.
- You find yourself hiding at work from your boss. You walk on eggshells and are in constant fight-or-flight mode.
- Your stress level is permeating your entire life.
- You spend more time and energy thinking about office politics or strategizing to survive your boss than you do on your work.
- Your self-esteem and self-confidence have plummeted.
- You are living in fear, stress, or unhappiness.
- You've tried to make it work, and nothing makes it work.
- You are ready to shift from surviving into thriving.

From Frying Pan to Fire

What keeps people working for horrible bosses? What keeps people from leaving those difficult situations? What keeps us from taking control of our own career destinies? All too often, we stay too long because of two competing emotional drivers: fear and hope. Both of these drivers may impair our decision making. Let's talk first about fear. What do people fear? Loss, failure, and the unknown. We are afraid to make a change and are fearful of our ability to succeed in making a change. We fear the potential fire of our choices.

To illustrate, here are common responses we hear from workshop attendees on why they stay working for horrible bosses or at dead-end jobs:

- I don't have time to look for a new job.
- The devil I know is better than the devil I don't. What if I make a bad choice?
- I really like my job. Why should I have to leave?
- I need the salary. I can't afford to take a pay cut.
- This is the only job in my field in the area.
- I don't want to let down my colleagues.
- I don't want to lose the status that my job or company affords me.
- The job market is too tight. There aren't any other jobs.
- I have too much debt to change jobs.
- I don't want to lose the amazing benefits and perks – health insurance, retirement plans, flexible work, etc.
- There aren't any good places to work. Everywhere is the same.
- I've invested so much that I don't want to start over in a new organization.
- This job pays too well to leave.
- I sent out some résumés, but nothing came from it.
- I don't have the skills to get a different job.
- I feel guilty because someone recommended me or helped me get this job.
- I don't know what else I would do.
- If I leave, then my boss wins.
- Things might get better.
- I am not a quitter.

Changing jobs is hard. Changing jobs is scary. You might make a mistake. You might not find the perfect job. You might not find a job that pays as well. Yes, yes, yes – all of your fears are *valid* – but they may not be *true*. You won't know until you explore them. If you find yourself miserable and making any of these excuses for staying, I encourage you to truly interrogate your reality. Many of those statements are based more on fear that objective reality. This is when our fear impairs our decision-making capability.

While fear is a huge factor that keeps people inert, for many of us, it is hope that springs eternal. We are optimistic; we think the next day has to be better. At some point, the boss will change her ways, the organization will take some action, things will improve! We know that silver lining is there somewhere and we are going to find it. There has to be a pot of gold at the end of this horror-house rainbow.

Hope and optimism are wonderful qualities. They are emotional drivers of many successful people. They are the emotions that researchers say are key for surviving catastrophes. Hope and optimism are often the differentiators between those who survive a terrible situation and those who don't. But we are not talking about being lost at sea or stuck in a POW camp. We're talking about a 9-to-5 job in a first-world country. If the best you can hope for is to survive your boss, then I hope some of the strategies in this book will help you.

However, if you are tired of just surviving and you want the chance to start thriving, then I encourage you to use that hope (or fear) to consider another choice. Try to understand the opportunity cost for that choice. You are choosing to survive or to thrive.

It's the Economy, Stupid

When Bill Clinton ran for president in 1992, his campaign strategist James Carville helped lead a successful campaign by reminding everyone that the campaign was about the economy, which resulted in the famous phrase, "It's the economy, stupid." If you are reluctant to leave or are not sure if it's the right move, then I recommend that you view your decision through a simple economic analysis. It's economics 101, stupid!

For some, the reluctance to quit stems from fallacious economic decision making. Put simply, human beings often suffer confusion between sunk costs versus opportunity costs. For those of you who don't remember (or, in my case, slept through) your Econ 101 class, this basic economic principle goes like this: *Sunk costs* refer to resources (time, energy, money, etc.) that were incurred in the past. These costs are *irrecoverable*. You cannot get them back. *Opportunity costs* refer to the future. It's understanding the benefit, profit, or reward that is lost or gained by selecting one alternative over another. It is the gain that could be realized if a resource (you!) were put to its next best use. Simply put, opportunity cost is what we give up or gain from "the road not taken." In other words, staying in a position with a boss who makes you miserable means you are losing twice: you are doubling down on your entire cost structure by adding your sunk cost (time spent in that position) with your opportunity cost (the cost of future happiness, growth, and joy). From an economic standpoint, it is idiocy. Very often, quitting is the smart move.

This point is illustrated in Eric's story.

Real-Life Story

Eric was director of development for a local chapter of a national non-profit. He loved his job and was good at it. In fact, he was the most successful fundraiser of all the chapters. Things were great until his chapter hired a new executive director. "I was very excited about Nancy becoming our new executive director," he said. "The national office allowed me to be part of the search process and I was Nancy's biggest supporter. When she started, she said she would be a hands-off boss and would look to each of us to be a leader of our own department. She said that she would be there to advise, but mostly wanted to learn from us. That lasted about a day. Quickly, she became an emotional bully, an extreme Micromanager, and very impulsive. Everything was a gut feeling for her. She vacillated from giving us the cold shoulder to constantly looking over our shoulder. We never knew who she was going to be from one day to the next. She even told us that she was very sensitive to being 'managed up' and will buck the trend if we try. It was one of the craziest situations I have ever seen.

"I tried really hard to make it work. I'm usually good at managing up, so I tried every strategy I could think of. The national organization tried to help – they wanted me to stay – but they

(continued)

(continued)

weren't willing to choose me over Nancy. The search for her was too expensive and time consuming. They kept telling me that they believed I could somehow make it work. While other members of the senior team saw the writing on the wall and were jumping ship, I was committed to sticking it out. I was attached to the mission and to the fund-raising program that I had built. I had spent too much time, energy, passion, and creativity in that organization to walk away. Even though I was miserable, I wanted to stick it out."

Eric's past experience, time, and energy put into the organization were sunk costs. That time and energy were already spent. Sunk costs are irrecoverable. His opportunity costs for choosing to stay were happiness and success. In other words, Eric was choosing merely to survive when he could have chosen to thrive. Eric was never going to be happy working for Nancy. Nancy was never going to let Eric be successful. Staying in his current position just didn't make emotional or economic sense.

"It took me way too long to realize that by choosing to stay and work for Nancy – who wasn't going anywhere – that I was passing up an opportunity to find success and happiness elsewhere. My attachment to making the most out of my past effort was blocking me from stepping into my future."

That last sentence is key: The attachment to making the most out of past efforts (sunk costs) blocks people from the opportunity to be successful.

A Poisoned Well Is a Poisoned Well

If you are still holding out that you can change your boss or that you can tough it out, please remember Sara's poisoned well analogy in the Narcissist chapter: *You go to the well and discover the water is poisoned. So, you think, what can I do? I can bring a different cup, so you bring a second cup, and then you try a third cup. You take a different route to the well. You try all kinds of different ways to drink the poisoned water. But when the water is poisoned, the water is poisoned. It doesn't matter what path you take and it doesn't matter what cup you have. The water is poisoned. You can't drink the water.*

If you are in a poisoned job, with a poisoned boss, then you must give yourself permission to save yourself. At some point, you need to walk away. Your horrible boss is not going to change. Take the power back. Stop trying to drink the poison.

You have to know when to walk away.

The Right Way to Quit

Once you make the decision to quit please try to do it gracefully, strategically, and safely.

First of all, resist the urge to go out in a blaze of anger and curse words. While this may feel great at the time, it isn't a good idea. You want to leave as professionally as possible. Here are a few tips and guidelines:

1. **Line up your next move.**
   If possible try to have an employment plan before you leave. Conventional wisdom and employment research shows that it is usually easier to find a job when you already have a job. Potential employers like to hire people who are already employed because it sends a message that you are a valuable commodity. "Stealing" you away makes them feel smart. It also shows that you are a serious worker, one who can commit to an employer. The choice to leave before finding another job is one that only you can make. As a practical Midwesterner, I would have a hard time myself free floating. However, I know plenty of people who have made the leap without a safety net. It really depends on your personal preference and economic conditions. And if your parents will let you move into their basement.

2. **Do not burn bridges.**
   Leave on the best circumstances possible. The world is smaller than you think. You never know where, when, or if you are going to run into your former boss or coworkers. Protect your professional image and brand by leaving gracefully and professionally.

3. **Give your boss and your organization proper notice.**

   The standard for most industries is two weeks. If you want to give a little more that is up to you, but try not to give them less if you can help it. If you are in a white collar job, you should write a resignation letter and tell your supervisor – in person – that you are leaving. Try to contain your glee when you do this.

   Don't forget, letters of resignation often end up in employee files and might be used if your former boss is ever called for a reference. Make sure your letter is professional and positive.

4. **Be as succinct and positive as possible.**

   Try not to say much more than you are leaving. If you can muster it, try to emphasize the positive aspects of your experience in the job. Avoid being negative or accusatory if you can – there's no point to it now. It's not like your supervisor is going to suddenly realize what an ass he or she has been. Try something like, "Bob, I wanted to let you know in person that I am submitting my two-week resignation. My time here at XYZ has been illuminating and interesting. While I'm grateful for the experience, I have decided it is time for me to move on to my next professional opportunity." Bam. Like a Band-Aid. Just rip it off.

5. **Create a transition timeline.**

   Clearly articulate your plans for transition. Be clear about what you are going to do before you leave and stick to it. If you promise to finish projects, then finish them. Don't bite off more than you can chew, but don't leave things on the plate that you promised to take care of. Leave your boss and your team fully updated on the status of projects, etc.

6. **Set up your successor for success.**

   Do the best you can to make it easy for the next person to find things, pick up where you left off, etc. Resist the urge to leave secret notes that say "Get out, now!" in the desk drawers.

7. **Be prepared to leave before your time.**

   If your boss is Truly Terrible, she may kick you out the minute you give notice. *Before* you give notice, make sure you have organized your personal belongings, contact information, important papers, commendations, etc. Be sure you are able to return all company property promptly and properly. If you have any company equipment, make sure you turn it back in and get proper documentation stating that you've returned it. The last thing you want is someone claiming you've stolen anything.

8. **Know what they owe you.**

Depending on your organization, they may owe you unused sick leave or vacation time. Be sure you know how to cash out or transfer company benefits, retirement plans, health insurance, etc. A visit to the HR department is helpful.

9. **Do the exit interview.**

If offered an exit interview with HR, be honest but tactful. Who knows? Maybe if HR hears enough horror stories about your horrible boss, something might change. And sometimes pigs fly. Don't count on it, but don't be afraid to express the difficulty of working for Mr. or Ms. Horrible. Just keep it professional, rational, and factual. And of course, show appreciation for the experience.

10. **Say goodbye.**

Take the time to say goodbye to your colleagues. Relationships are currency in the working world. Keep your relationships the best you can.

11. **Do not bad-mouth.**

Never bad-mouth your current boss during interviews with potential employers. They don't know you. They don't know your boss. All they see is someone talking badly about his boss. The potential employer won't see a workplace refugee, they will see a complaining malcontent. They will wonder what you might say about *them* when you leave. Believe me, even if your potential employer digs in for the gossip, it will backfire on you. While I would love to hear your story about your horrible boss, I would never hire someone who bad-mouths their current employer, and I don't know any other leader who would either.

12. **Even then, don't bad-mouth.**

Try not to bad-mouth your old boss even *after* you get the new job, at least until you've developed a deep well of trust with your new employer. I once had a great employee who waited six months before he told me his tale of woe with his former boss. I'm glad he waited. Had he told me sooner, part of me would have harbored some doubt and suspicion about him. It was a smart move on his part to wait until we had built a huge well of trust and respect and I was able to witness his amazing work habits. Try to keep your venting in your new organization close to the vest, and share only with close and trusted colleagues and friends.

Strategy Recap

- Get your ducks in a row before you quit – get your personal belongings together, gather any company equipment, and know what they owe you.
- Give proper notice.
- Do not burn bridges.
- Be as professional and respectful as possible.
- Say goodbye to your team and colleagues.
- Be gracious in the exit interview.
- Do not bad-mouth your terrible boss, at least not until you have developed a solid, trusting relationship with your new boss or colleagues.

22

Bonus Tips – 50 Ways to Manage Your Manager

"Every success story is a tale of constant adaption, revision, and change."

—Richard Branson

Managing up is a true art form that has many facets, shapes, and configurations. While the bulk of this book explored managing up based on specific personality traits and behaviors, the list below contains our top 50 tips for managing up *normal, everyday* bosses. Consider them the basic tenets of managing up. Enjoy, and good luck!

1. **Build the relationship/foster a partnership.**
   Take the time to really build a relationship. Get to know your boss. Learn about who he is. Learn about what she's done. Have coffee now and then. Show him that you share his goals. Show her that you can be counted on to achieve organizational priorities. Be a human being.

2. **Be a professional at all times.**
   No matter what your boss does, you should always approach work in a professional manner. Take yourself and your job seriously.

3. **Bring solutions not problems.**
   Always hand your boss proposed solutions instead of only problems. In fact, you should never bring a problem to your boss

without at least one proposed solution. Presenting options is even better. Show your boss that you are a self-sufficient, proactive problem solver.

4. **No surprises.**

Never give your boss surprises. Make her aware of everything that is important to her job, so that she can avoid surprising *her* boss.

5. **Be humble.**

A little respectful humility goes a long way. Don't approach your boss with a sense of entitlement. Be willing to learn and take on menial tasks to prove you are a team player.

6. **Cut some slack.**

Remember that your boss is only human and may be under a lot more pressure than you realize. He is not necessarily trying to make your life difficult. He may be doing the best he can with what he has.

7. **Be honest.**

Always admit your errors. Most bosses are willing to tolerate mistakes as part of the learning process. Own up to them with grace and a commitment to do better.

8. **Respect your boss's time.**

When you walk into her office, be clear and prepared. In addition to managing you (and others) your boss most likely has her own tasks to accomplish. Know what you need from her and get out.

9. **Accept and adapt.**

Don't try to change your boss. Don't resist who he is. Study his preferences and conform to them whenever possible.

10. **Build and compensate.**

Recognize your boss's strengths and build on them. Recognize her weaknesses and compensate for them. If your boss takes terrible notes or forgets to recap action items in a meeting, do it for her. You will be doing your boss, yourself, and the organization a favor.

11. **Align your priorities.**

Make sure your priorities are aligned with the priorities of your boss and the organization. Failure to adjust to shifting priorities can derail success. Never make assumptions about your boss's goals. Be very clear about how you can help your boss achieve objectives.

12. **Make a new plan, Stan.**
    If your current strategies for managing up aren't working, try something different. If your boss isn't responding well to your mode of communication, try a different mode. If your boss doesn't seem to appreciate your contributions, find different contributions. Keep trying! Don't be one and done.

13. **Take feedback well.**
    Develop skills for receiving feedback, both positive and constructive. Have a growth mindset when it comes to criticism. Adopt a learning attitude and request more specific information when feedback is vague. Feedback is a gift, even when critical. And the proper response to feedback – even critical – is always "thank you."

14. **Stay on their radar.**
    Communicate (in some small way) to the boss every day that you can. Even if it is just to say hello or good night. Don't be a pest. Just build a relationship and stay on her radar.

15. **Learn their perspective.**
    Understand (and appreciate) the world from your boss's point of view. Put yourself in his shoes. Your boss may not always be right, but he does set the agenda.

16. **Make your boss's life easy.**
    Find ways to make your manager's life just a little easier. Be on the lookout for opportunities every day – big or little – that can make a difference.

17. **Don't whine.**
    If your boss is snippy, snappy, or rude with every now and then, let it go. Everyone has a bad day once in a while. Don't be a crybaby.

18. **Be a "can-do" employee.**
    Take on challenges. Deliver on projects with a positive attitude. If your boss asks for help in a group setting, be the first to volunteer.

19. **Show appreciation.**
    Say "thank you" whenever you can. Everyone appreciates being appreciated. A little gratitude goes a long way.

20. **Pay them a compliment from time to time.**
    Managing is hard work. Few managers ever get feedback on their managing. Remember that everyone appreciates a little professional kind word or compliment now and then.

21. **Share the whole truth.**

    If you have information that your boss needs to know or might need to know, bring it to her even if it might not be good news. Don't only share the good news.

22. **Acknowledge the good bits.**

    When you're negative about your boss, the tendency is to focus on her worst traits and failings. This is neither positive for your work happiness nor your prospects for success in your organization. Keep your mind open to seeing the positive traits as well.

23. **Don't lie, cheat, or steal.**

    Maintain high ethical standards, even if your boss doesn't.

24. **Request, don't complain.**

    Inside every complaint is a request. Find it and make it.

25. **Make your requests effective.**

    Bosses aren't mind readers. When you make a request be clear about what you are requesting, what it would look like, and why it is important. Even better, show how your requests are aligned with both your boss's goals and priorities and those of your organization. Frame your request as a win-win-win.

26. **Do the job you were hired to do.**

    Know your role and your duties. Be clear about what is expected of you and deliver those results on time. Don't make short shrift of the annoying tasks in favor of the more engaging tasks.

27. **Under-promise and over-deliver.**

    This age-old maxim is age-old for a reason. It works. Keep your commitments and deliver stellar results ahead of deadlines. Set yourself up for success and not failure.

28. **Know what really matters to your boss and give it to her.**

    Is your boss big on punctuality? Then show up on time. Does your boss want to get promoted? Then find ways to help her climb the ladder. Does your boss want you to use the Oxford comma? Then learn what that is, and use it.

29. **Be aware of their hot buttons and pet peeves.**

    Learn what they are and avoid them, even if you think they are stupid. Does your boss flip out when you don't use the Oxford comma? For goodness's sake, then use the Oxford comma!

30. **Request feedback.**

    If you aren't getting feedback, ask for it. Be specific about the kind of feedback you want and why you need it. Make it easy for the boss to know what you need. And, for heaven's sake, when you get it, make sure you "hear" it and take action. Don't get defensive (even if it is wrong). Try to find the golden nugget.

31. **Don't backstab.**

    Don't go over your boss's head or behind his back. Nobody likes the blindside. Especially bosses.

32. **Anticipate needs.**

    Pay attention to your boss's goals and deliverables and be proactive about helping. For example, if you know your boss has to give quarterly sales projections to the board of directors, be proactive about getting those to her well before she asks. Show that you are paying attention and are staying ahead of the curve.

33. **Be enthusiastic about your duties.**

    Nobody wants to work with a Debbie Downer.

34. **Turn to the team.**

    Notice what others are doing that works with your boss and doesn't work. Do what works, don't do what doesn't. And if you see a team member doing something you know doesn't work, for goodness's sake, help him out. Your boss and your team will be much happier if everyone is rowing in the same direction. Don't forget the expression, "One bad apple . . . "

35. **Make your boss look good.**

    The truth is that if your boss looks good, you will as well. It's the art of association. If your boss looks bad, then guess what? That will reflect badly on you, too. A high tide raises all boats.

36. **Keep your boss informed.**

    Don't assume your boss knows about all your accomplishments. Take the time to keep her up to date and posted on your activities and accomplishments.

37. **Use "we" not "I."**

    When talking about departmental successes to your boss's boss or other organizational leaders, make sure you share the credit. He will notice.

38. **Use "I" not "you."**

When discussing your needs, wants, and expectations with your boss, make sure you frame your requests based on *your* needs, as in "I'd like to learn more about X project" instead of "You need to tell me more about X project." It's a subtle difference and it works.

39. **Don't "Yes, but" your boss.**

Nobody likes to be "Yes, butted." Using the word "but" after the word "yes" totally negates the yes. The result? People don't feel heard, they just feel butted. And when people feel butted, they get defensive and argumentative. So, the next time you want to "Yes, but," try substituting "Yes, and" instead. It's magic.

40. **Don't be a jerk.**

Even if your boss is one. The world has too many jerks as it is. Don't add to the problem.

41. **Honor your commitments.**

If you say you are going to do something, do it. Don't leave your boss hanging. If you find that you can't make a deadline or meet a commitment, discuss options or a plan B with your boss directly and proactively *before* the deadline.

42. **Challenge appropriately.**

Managing up isn't about sucking up. If you have a different perspective, offer it respectfully and appropriately. This may take a bit of trial and error to figure out the best method and context. Try not to embarrass or weaken your boss in public settings.

43. **Be flexible.**

Organizations are constantly in flux. Priorities change. Goals shift. Urgent issues happen. Be flexible when you can and learn to adjust to ambiguity when necessary. Don't be the person who can't accept change.

44. **Discuss delegation.**

When your boss delegates a project, ask up front about his expectations, wants, and needs. Find out how much autonomy you have in the project, how much input he wants, and what kind of check-ins he needs. Don't guess – ask.

45. **Consider the culture.**

Your boss doesn't exist in a vacuum. And neither do you. Is your boss's behavior indicative and reflective of the organizational culture or is she an anomaly? Look for ways in which your boss successfully navigates the culture and emulate those behaviors. Be aware of ways your boss clashes with the culture and avoid those practices.

46. **Speak up!**

Make sure your boss knows how to best use your skills and talents. Are you a whiz with words? Let your boss know. Are you great at networking? Let your boss know. Are you a spreadsheet queen? Let your boss know. Most importantly, let your boss know how your strengths, talents, and skills can help her and the organization be successful.

47. **Develop external awareness.**

Be aware of things going on within your organization, the world, and your industry. Staying on top of external realities can help you be more effective in your job.

48. **Manage yourself first.**

Then your boss. Take responsibility for always bringing your best.

49. **Defend, don't bad-mouth.**

Defend your boss to others in public the best you can. The walls have ears and you don't want your bad-mouthing to get back to your boss. Try to publicly defend your boss's decisions, even the ones with which you may disagree. Learn the art of diplomacy. Learn to say things like, "Yes, that was a surprising decision and I am sure we can find a way to make it work."

50. **Have the conversation.**

Not sure what is important to your boss? Ask her. Not sure what his priorities are? Ask him. Not sure what her communication preferences are? Ask her. Not sure what he expects of you? Don't guess. Ask.

Index